W. W. Jacobs
Amelia B. Edwards
E. A. Poe
Bram Stoker

Gothic SHORT STORIES

Retold by **Peter Foreman** and **Kenneth Brodey**
Activities by **Kenneth Brodey** and **Peter Foreman**

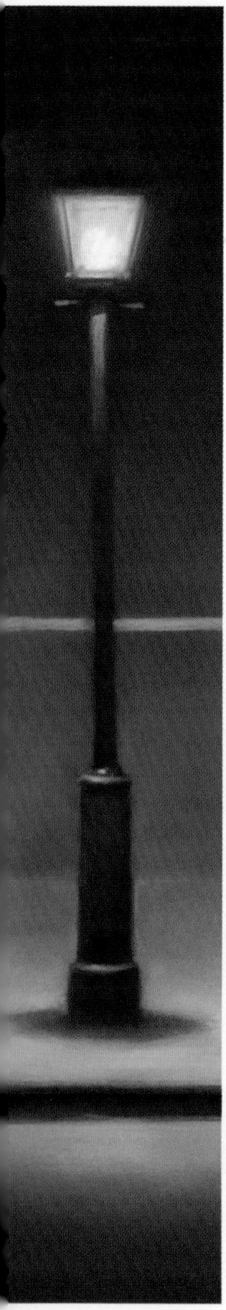

Editors: Victoria Bradshaw, Richard Elliott
Design and art direction: Nadia Maestri
Computer graphics: Simona Corniola
Illustrations: Gianni De Conno
Picture research: Laura Lagomarsino

First edition : May 2004

Picture credits

The Bridgeman Art Library: 66; NTPL / Matthew Antrobus: 67;
© Bettman / CONTRASTO: 68.

We would be happy to receive your comments and suggestions, and give you any other information concerning our material.
editorial@blackcat-cideb.com
www.blackcat-cideb.com
www.cideb.it

CISQ CISQCERT
TEXTBOOKS AND TEACHING MATERIALS
The quality of the publisher's design, production and sales processes has been certified to the standard of
UNI EN ISO 9001

ISBN 978-88-530-0175-7 Book
ISBN 978-88-530-0176-4 Book + CD

Printed in Italy by Litoprint, Genoa

Contents

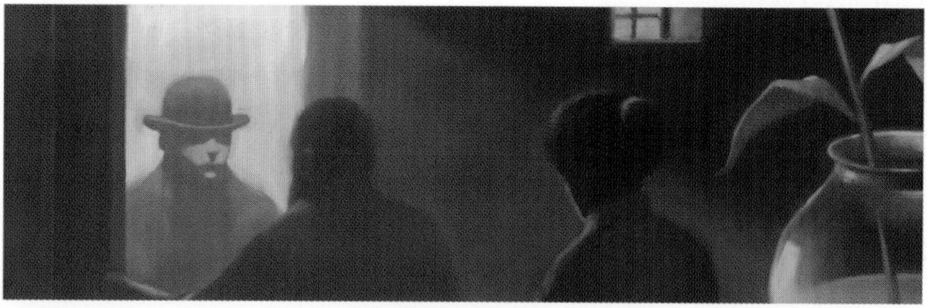

FCE First Certificate in English Examination-style exercises

T: GRADE 8 Trinity-style exercises (Grade 8)

This story is recorded in full.

These symbols indicate the beginning and end of the extracts linked to the listening activities.

Notes on *the Authors*

W. W. Jacobs (1863-1943)

William Wymark Jacobs was born and grew up near the River Thames in London. Although he wrote several novels, he is mainly known for his short stories, many of which depict horrifying tales of terror and the macabre. Jacobs' unique appeal lies in his ability to build suspense by taking an everyday situation and adding unexpected elements of superstition and dread. 'The Monkey's Paw', Jacobs' most famous short story was first published in 1902.

Amelia B. Edwards (1831-92)

Amelia B. Edwards was a novelist and Egyptologist. Between 1855 and 1880 she wrote for several magazines and published eight novels and many short stories. After visiting Egypt in 1873-4, she began to study the country's ancient history and helped to establish the Egypt Exploration Fund in 1882. On her death in 1892 she left her library and collections on Egyptology to University College London.

E. A. Poe (1809-49)

Edgar Allan Poe is famous for his short stories of terror, and more particularly for being the inventor of the modern detective story. Born in Boston, at the age of two his mother died. He was then brought up by merchant John Allan. He started writing seriously as

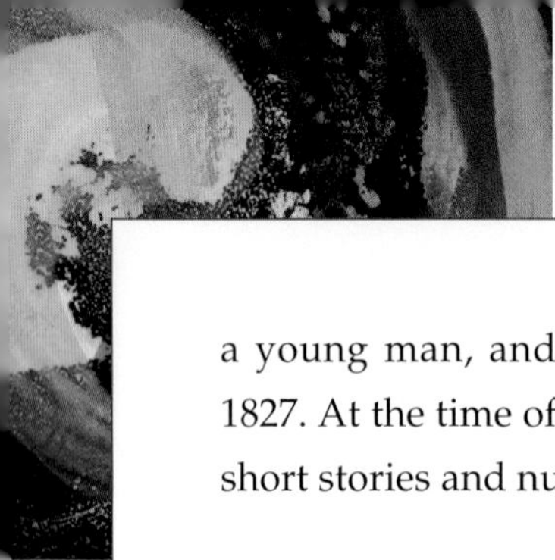

a young man, and his first collection of poetry was published in 1827. At the time of his death, at the age of 40, he had written over 70 short stories and numerous poems.

Bram Stoker (1847-1912)

Abraham Stoker was an Irish writer and theatre manager. Born in Dublin, he studied law and science at Trinity College. At first he worked in the Irish Civil Service, but in 1878 he became the business manager of the great actor Sir Henry Irving. While he worked with Irving, organizing the Lyceum Theatre in London, he wrote novels and short stories. *Dracula* (1897), his most famous work, is now a classic of horror fiction.

1 Who did what?

Answer the following questions.

Who:

a. left an important collection of books and objects to a university? ....

b. wasn't born in the British Isles? ....

c. worked for the government? ....

d. wrote novels, but is better-known for his/her short stories? ....

e. was particularly interested in ancient history? ....

f. took the name of a foster parent? ....

g. helped run a theatre? ....

The MONKEY'S PAW[1]

by **W. W. Jacobs**

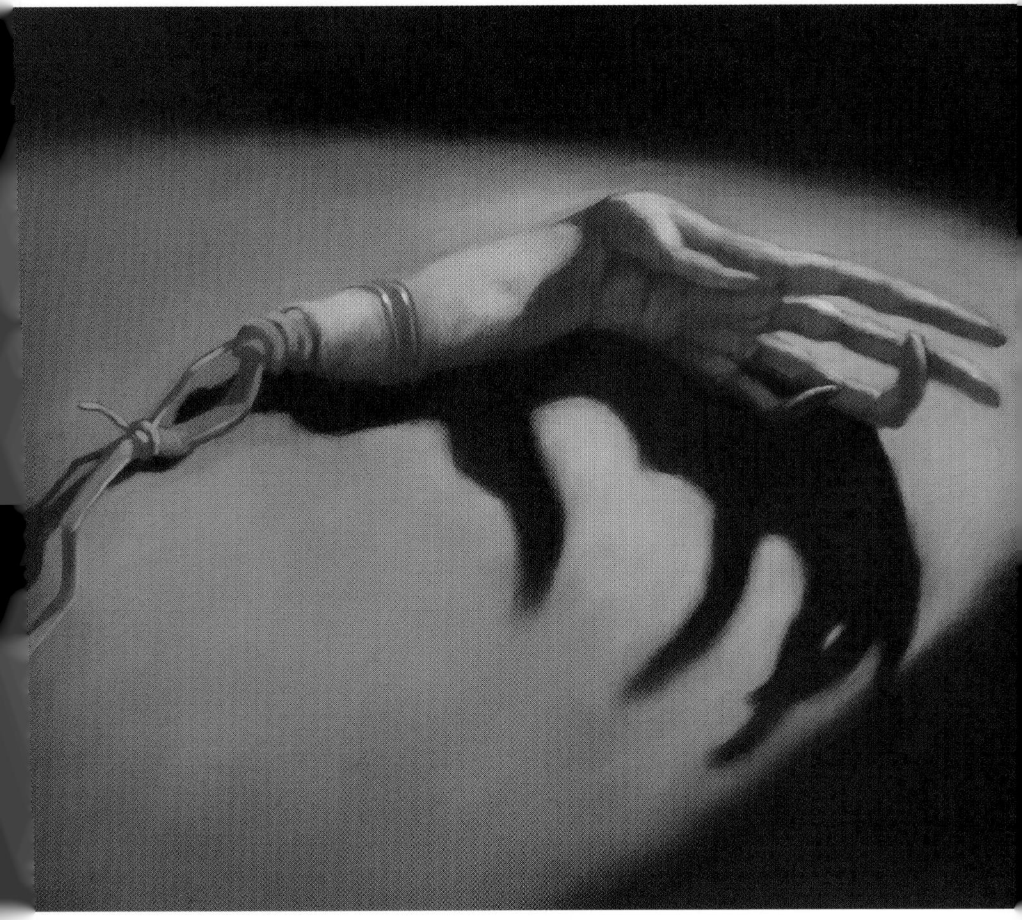

1. **paw** : foot of an animal.

Before you read

1 If you could have three wishes, what would they be? Write them in order of importance.

1. ....
2. ....
3. ....

2 The Irish writer Oscar Wilde wrote, 'In this world there are only two tragedies. One is not getting what one wants, and the other is getting it.'

a. What do you think Wilde meant by this?

b. Do you think there is any truth in it?

c. If one of your three wishes came true, is there any way that this could bring you sadness and suffering?

FCE **3 Listen to the beginning of Part One and complete the sentences with a word or a phrase.**

2

1 The weather outside was ....

2 Mr White and .... were playing a game of chess.

3 Sergeant Major Morris was an old, well-built man with small bright eyes and ....

4 The Sergeant Major began to talk after he had had ....

5 The Sergeant Major went to India .... ago.

6 The Sergeant Major told Mr White that he was .... where he was.

PART ONE

Outside, the night was cold and wet but a fire burned brightly in the small living room of Laburnum Villa, where Mr White and his son Herbert were playing chess. [1] Mrs White, a white-haired old lady, sat knitting [2] by the fire, occasionally commenting on the game.

'Listen to the wind,' said Mr White. He had made a serious mistake and wanted to distract his son's attention so that he wouldn't see it.

'I'm listening,' said his son, concentrating on the chessboard.

'I shouldn't think he'll come tonight,' said the father, his hand over the board.

'Checkmate,' [3] replied the son.

'That's the trouble with living here,' Mr White shouted with unexpected violence. 'Of all the wet, isolated places this is the

1. **chess** : a board game for two players who move their pieces according to particular rules.
2. **knitting** ['nɪtɪŋ] : making something from wool.
3. **Checkmate** : expression used in chess. It means that Herbert has won the game.

worst. The path is a bog [1] and the road's a river, but I suppose people don't care because only two houses in the road are occupied.'

'Don't worry, dear,' said his wife. 'Perhaps you'll win the next one.'

Mr White looked up suddenly and saw mother and son look at each other quickly. He hid a guilty smile in his thin grey beard.

'There he is,' said Herbert, hearing the gate shut loudly and heavy footsteps coming to the door.

The old man stood up hurriedly and went to open the door. He came back with a tall, well-built man who had small, bright eyes and a red face.

'Sergeant Major Morris,' said Mr White, introducing him.

The officer shook hands, sat by the fire, and watched contentedly as Mr White got out some whisky and glasses. After three drinks the soldier's eyes became brighter and he began to talk. The family listened with great interest to this visitor from distant lands while he spoke of his courageous adventures and his experiences of wars, plagues and strange nations.

'Twenty-one years ago, when he went away, he was just a boy in the warehouse,' [2] said Mr White to his wife and son. 'Now look at him.'

'It doesn't seem to have hurt him,' Mrs White agreed politely.

'I'd like to go to India myself,' said the old man, 'just to look round a bit, you know.'

'You're better here where you are,' said the Sergeant Major, shaking his head. He put down his empty glass, sighed, and shook his head again.

END

1. **bog** : area of soft, wet ground. Mr White means the path is impassable.
2. **warehouse** : building where goods or commodities are kept.

'I'd like to see those old temples, and fakirs and jugglers,' [1] continued Mr White. 'What was that about a monkey's paw or something you started telling me about the other day, Morris?'

'Nothing,' said the other quickly. 'Nothing worth hearing anyway.'

'Monkey's paw?' said Mrs White curiously.

'Well, it's just a bit of what you might call magic,' said the soldier casually.

But the three listeners were looking at him eagerly. Mr White filled his glass for him.

'It's just an ordinary little paw to look at,' said Sergeant Major Morris, taking it from his pocket.

Mrs White moved back with a disgusted look, but her son examined it curiously.

'And what's so special about it?' Mr White asked. He took it from his son, examined it, and put it on the table.

'An old fakir put a spell on it. [2] He was a very holy man and he wanted to show that fate ruled people's lives, and that to interfere with fate only caused deep sadness. He put a spell on it so that three separate men could each have three wishes from it.'

His manner was so impressive that the others realized their careless laughter was not appropriate.

'Well, why don't you have three wishes?' said Mr White.

The soldier looked at him as if he were a foolish boy. 'I have,' he said quietly, and his red face whitened.

'And did your three wishes really come true?' asked Mrs White.

'Yes.'

1. **fakirs** ['fakɪəz] **and jugglers** : holy men and street entertainers.
2. **put a spell on it** : spoke words that gave the paw magical powers.

D

'And has nobody else wished?' the old lady went on.

'The first man had his three wishes, yes. I don't know what the first two wishes were but the third was for death. That's how I got the paw.'

He spoke so seriously that everybody became quiet.

'If you've had your three wishes, the paw is no good to you now,' said Mr White at last. 'Why do you keep it?'

The soldier shook his head and said slowly, 'Oh, just for interest, I suppose. I had some idea of selling it but I don't think I will. It has caused enough trouble already. Anyway, people won't buy it. Some think it's all a fairy story, [1] and those who believe it want to try it before paying me.'

'If you could have another three wishes,' said old Mr White, looking interestedly at him, 'would you have them?'

'I don't know, I don't know.'

Then he took the paw and suddenly threw it on the fire. With an astonished cry Mr White bent down and pulled it out quickly.

'Better let it burn,' said the soldier.

'If you don't want it, give it to me, Morris.'

'No. I threw it on the fire. If you keep it, don't then say that it is my fault. Be sensible – throw it on the fire again!'

But, examining his new possession closely, Mr White shook his head. 'How do you do it?' he asked Morris.

'Hold it up in your right hand and wish aloud,' was the reply. 'But I warn you of the consequences.'

'It sounds like the *Arabian Nights*,' [2] Mrs White said as she

1. **fairy story** : children's story, fable.
2. **Arabian Nights** : collection of stories written in Arabic. They include the stories of 'Aladdin' and 'Sinbad the Sailor'.

began to prepare the dinner. 'Why don't you wish for four pairs of hands for me?'

Laughing, her husband took the talisman [1] from his pocket to make the wish but with a look of alarm the Sergeant Major caught his arm.

'If you must wish,' he said aggressively, 'wish for something reasonable.'

So Mr White put it back in his pocket and they all sat down to dinner. The talisman was partly forgotten for the rest of the evening as the soldier continued telling them about his exciting adventures in India. When he had gone, Mr White said that the story of the monkey's paw was probably untrue, like all the other stories Morris had told them.

'Did you give him anything for it?' Mrs White asked him.

'Oh, just a bit of money. He didn't want it but I made him take it. And he tried to persuade me again to throw the thing away.'

'Of course we will!' said Herbert ironically. 'God, we're going to be rich and famous and happy! Wish that you were an emperor, father, to begin with. Then mother won't order you around.'

Mrs White pretended to be angry at this and chased him round the table, while Mr White looked at the paw doubtfully.

'I don't know what to wish for and that's a fact,' he said slowly. 'It seems to me I've got all I want.'

'If you could finish paying for the house you'd be quite happy, wouldn't you?' Herbert said. 'Wish for two hundred pounds, then. That'll just do it.'

His father, in an embarrassed way, held up the talisman as

1. **talisman** : object believed to have magic powers (here, the monkey's paw).

Herbert, with a wink [1] at his mother, sat down at the piano and played a few solemn notes.

'I wish for two hundred pounds,' said the old man distinctly.

As Herbert played a loud, dramatic chord the old man suddenly cried out in a trembling voice. His wife and son ran towards him.

'It moved,' he cried, glancing with disgust at the object on the floor. 'As I wished, it twisted [2] in my hand like a snake.'

'Well, I don't see the money,' said Herbert, picking it up. 'And I am sure I never will.'

'It must have been your imagination,' said Mrs White, looking anxiously at her husband.

He shook his head. 'It doesn't matter — nobody's hurt. But it gave me a shock.'

They sat down by the fire. While the men smoked their pipes the wind outside blew harder than ever and the old man became nervous at the sound of a door banging noisily upstairs as it closed. An unusual and depressing silence fell on the family. Then the old couple stood up to go upstairs to bed.

'You'll probably find the money in a big bag in the middle of your bed,' Herbert joked as he said goodnight to them.

He sat alone in the darkness, looking absently into the fire and seeing faces in it. One face was so horrible and monkey-like he stared [3] at it in amazement. When he realized he was still holding the monkey's paw he quickly put it down and with a little shiver wiped his hand on his coat. [4] Then he went up to bed.

1. **wink** : opening and closing one eye quickly.
2. **twisted** : turned spasmodically.
3. **stared** : looked for a long time.
4. **with... coat** : trembled with fear and cleaned his hand on his coat.

Go back to the text

FCE **1 Choose the best answer A, B, C or D.**

1 Mr White told his son to listen to the wind because

A ☐ it was making a strange sound.

B ☐ he did not want his son to see the mistake he had made.

C ☐ he was worried that the Sergeant Major wouldn't come because of the bad weather.

D ☐ it made him think how isolated they were.

2 Mr White suddenly complained about how isolated his house was because

A ☐ he was angry that nobody cared about his house.

B ☐ he was feeling tired.

C ☐ he had just lost the chess game.

D ☐ he was sorry that he had bought that house.

3 The fakir put a spell on the monkey's paw because

A ☐ he wanted to make money.

B ☐ he wanted to show people that it was possible to interfere with fate.

C ☐ he wanted to show people that is was impossible to interfere with fate.

D ☐ he wanted to show people that they should not try to interfere with fate.

4 How did Sergeant Major Morris get the monkey's paw?

A ☐ He bought it from the fakir.

B ☐ He bought it from the previous owner.

C ☐ The previous owner died.

D ☐ He found it.

5 Mr White found it difficult to decide what to wish for because

A ☐ he felt that he didn't really need anything.

B ☐ he wasn't really convinced that Sergeant Major Morris had told him the truth.

C ☐ he wanted too many things.

D ☐ he wanted to be certain that what he wished for was reasonable.

6 Mr White was shocked when he made his wish because

A ☐ the paw moved in his hand.

B ☐ he suddenly saw a horrible monkey-like face looking at him from fire.

C ☐ Herbert was playing some dramatic music on the piano.

D ☐ the money didn't appear in front of him.

'Wish that you were an emperor, father'

After ***wish***, we use a verb in the **Past Simple** to talk about something that has a present or future meaning.
Look at these examples:

- I ***wish*** I ***had*** a house in the mountains. Then we could go skiing every weekend.
- I can't go on holiday because I have to work this summer. *I **wish** I **didn't have** to work.*

We often use ***were*** instead of ***was*** with all subjects after ***I wish***. This is more common in formal English.

- It's so hot today! *I **wish** it **weren't** so hot.*
- I ***wish*** I ***was*** able to swim, but I can't.

2 **Write a sentence with 'wish' and the verb given in brackets for the following situations.**

Example: I met this wonderful girl, but I don't have her address. (*know*)
I wish I knew her address.

a. My brother always helps me with my homework, but he is not at home today. (*be*)

b. Look at those people dancing. I am a terrible dancer. (*can*)

c. Our flat is on the fifth floor and we don't have a lift. (*be*)

d. I love the excitement of a big city, but our town is small and boring. (*live*)

e. We desperately need £200 to pay our rent. (*have*)

f. There is a great job in Spain, but I don't speak Spanish. (*can*)

The Monkey's Paw and Aladdin's Lamp

FCE **3** **For questions 1-10, read the text below. Use the word given in capitals at the end of each line to form a word that fits in the space in the same line. There is an example at the beginning.**

Just like the craze for Gothic novels in Europe in the	
1760s, fifty years (0) earlier........ a craze for the	EARLY
wonders of the Orient also began when a Frenchman	
Antoine Galland, published his French (1) ....,	TRANSLATE
of the (2) .... masterpiece, the *Arabian*	ORIENT
Nights, also known as *The Thousand and One Nights*.	
This huge (3) .... of wonderful stories seems	COLLECT
to have originally come from Persia and was finally	
translated into (4) .... in the 1400s.	ARAB
For the French of the early 1700s it opened up a	
world inhabited by men and women totally	
(5) .... themselves, where the rules of	LIKE
everyday living were suspended. They met	

(6) .... heroes such as Ali Baba, Aladdin and Sinbad the Sailor.	ASTONISH
Arabian Nights was soon followed by French versions of Turkish tales, Persian tales and (7) .... tales. Later it was also translated into English, but the (8) .... version in English was prepared in the 1880s by Richard Francis Burton. Burton, besides being an expert linguist, was also a famous (9) .... He was the first (10) .... to see the holy city of Mecca, and the great lakes of East Africa. He too, like Sergeant Major Morris, brought back magic from the East, but Burton's magic was literary.	CHINA DEFINITE EXPLORE EUROPE

Before you go on

FCE **1** **Listen to the beginning of Part Two and say whether the following statements are true (T) or false (F).** (3)

		T	F
1	Mrs White believed everything that Sergeant Major Morris had told them.	☐	☐
2	Mrs White could not understand how two hundred pounds could hurt them.	☐	☐
3	The Sergeant Major had said that the wishes happened in strange and unusual ways.	☐	☐
4	Mrs White was happy when the postman only brought a bill.	☐	☐
5	Mr White was no longer certain that the monkey's paw had moved in his hand.	☐	☐
6	The stranger who came to the Whites' house was badly dressed.	☐	☐
7	The stranger seemed to be afraid.	☐	☐

PART TWO

The next morning at breakfast Herbert laughed at his fears of the night before. The winter sun shone in the room, which looked very ordinary now, and the dirty, dried-up [1] little paw was still lying where he had thrown it carelessly.

'I suppose all old soldiers are the same,' Mrs White commented. 'Why did we listen to such nonsense? How could wishes be granted these days? And if they could, how could two hundred pounds hurt us?'

'Well, it could drop on father's head from the sky,' Herbert joked.

'Morris said the wishes happen naturally,' said his father, 'so you think they're just coincidences.'

'Don't spend any of the money before I come back,' Herbert said, going to the door.

His mother watched him walk down the road to work. Of course she didn't believe that the talisman could grant wishes,

1. **dried-up** : old and hard.

yet later that day she ran quickly to the door when the postman knocked and she was disappointed that it was only a bill.

'I expect Herbert will joke about it even more when he comes home,' she said at dinner.

'I expect he will,' said Mr White. 'But the thing moved in my hand — I swear it.'

'You thought it moved.'

'It moved, I tell you. I didn't think — what's the matter?'

His wife made no reply. She was watching the mysterious movements of a man outside in the street, who seemed to be trying to decide whether to open the gate and enter. She noticed that the stranger was well-dressed and wore a new silk hat. Three times he paused at the gate and walked away. The fourth time he stopped and put his hand on the gate, then suddenly opened it and walked up the path. Mrs White opened the front door and brought the stranger into the room. He seemed worried and uneasy, and looked at her from the corner of his eye. END

'I — was asked to call,' he began hesitantly. 'I am from Maw and Meggins.'

The old lady looked surprised. 'Is anything wrong?' she asked breathlessly. 'Has anything happened to Herbert? What is it?'

'Now don't worry,' said her husband. 'I'm sure he hasn't brought bad news. Have you, sir?' he concluded, looking hopefully at the visitor.

'I'm sorry —'

'Is he hurt?' demanded the mother wildly. [1]

The visitor looked down. 'Badly hurt,' he said quietly. 'But he's not in any pain.'

1. **wildly** : (here) emotionally.

'Oh, thank God, thank God for that!'

But the sinister meaning of the visitor's assurance suddenly became clear to the old lady and she looked at him. His face was turned away, confirming her worst fears. She caught her breath [1] and put her trembling hand on her husband's. There was a long silence.

'He became trapped in the machinery,' said the visitor in a low voice.

'Trapped in the machinery?' repeated Mr White in a daze. [2] He sat staring through the window, and taking his wife's hand, he pressed it as he used to when they were young lovers nearly forty years before. 'He was our only son,' he said to the visitor. 'It is hard.'

The other coughed [3] and walked slowly to the window. 'The firm wish me to express their sincere sympathy with you in your great loss,' he murmured, without looking at the old people.

There was no reply. Mrs White's face was pale, her eyes staring. The expression on Mr White's face was dark and serious.

'I have to tell you that Maw and Meggins do not hold themselves responsible for what has happened,' the visitor continued. 'But in consideration of your son's services they wish to give you a certain amount of money as compensation.'

Dropping his wife's hand, Mr White stood up and stared at the man with a look of horror.

'How much?' he said.

'Two hundred pounds.'

The old man smiled faintly, put out his hands like a blind man, and fell to the floor, unconscious.

1. **caught** [kɔːt] **her breath** [breθ] : breathed in suddenly.
2. **in a daze** : in a state of shock.
3. **coughed** [kɒft] : forced air out of his throat.

Go back to the text

1 Answer the following questions.

a. How did the living room look the morning after the Whites' exciting evening with Sergeant Major Morris?
b. What was Herbert's attitude towards the monkey's paw?
c. Who was the well-dressed stranger and why had he come to see the Whites?
d. How did Mrs White first understand that her son was dead?
e. How did Herbert die?
f. Why did the firm of Maw and Meggins decide to give the Whites some money?
g. Why did Mr White fall to the floor unconscious?

'The little paw was lying on the sideboard where he had thrown it'

We often use a verb in the **Past Perfect** alongside another verb in the **Past Simple** or **Past Continuous** to show that one past event happened before another.

Look at these examples:

- When he ***arrived*** at the Whites' house, it ***had*** already ***started*** to rain.
- Mr White ***fell*** on the floor unconscious after the man ***had told*** them the news.
- Mrs White believes that Herbert ***died*** because they ***had wished*** for £200.

2 **Read this short version of the story of Aladdin, and put the verbs from the box into the correct tense according to the context.**

be x 4	close	come x 3	die	explain	
find	give	learn	need	pretend	refuse
rub	save	tell x 2	walk		

Aladdin was the lazy son of a poor Chinese tailor. One day his uncle 0 ...came..... to see him after his father 1 .... He and Aladdin 2 .... around together, and his uncle 3 .... him many marvellous things. Finally, the uncle 4 .... to Aladdin that he 5 .... to visit him for a reason. There 6 .... a magic lamp in a cave and Aladdin's uncle 7 .... his help to get it. However, after they 8 .... the lamp, Aladdin 9 .... to give it to his uncle because his uncle 10 .... him that it was magical. His uncle 11 .... very angry and 12 .... the cave with Aladdin inside. It was then that Aladdin realized that the man was not really his uncle but an evil magician. In fact, he 13 .... a magician from Africa who 14 .... to be Aladdin's uncle. Years earlier the magician 15 .... that there 16 .... a wonderful treasure and a magic lamp in China, and that he could have this treasure only with the help of a boy named Aladdin.

Now Aladdin was alone in the cave and would die there. Fortunately, though, Aladdin 17 .... a ring that the magician 18 .... him. A genie 19 .... out and 20 .... Aladdin from certain death in the cave. Aladdin also learned that there was a genie in the magic lamp that would grant his wishes. In the end Aladdin, the lazy son of a poor tailor, married the Sultan's daughter.

What should they wish for now?

3 **Write a short composition saying what you think the Whites should do with the monkey's paw? Should they throw it away? Should they wish for something more? What? Justify your opinion.**

Before you go on

FCE **1** **Listen to the beginning of Part Three and choose the best answer A, B or C.**

1 Where did the Whites bury their son?

- **A** ☐ In an old family cemetery near their home.
- **B** ☐ In a large new cemetery two miles from their home.
- **C** ☐ In a small cemetery four miles from their home.

2 After their son's funeral, the Whites hardly talked because they

- **A** ☐ blamed each other.
- **B** ☐ were afraid of the monkey's paw.
- **C** ☐ had nothing to talk about.

3 Mrs White thought of using the monkey's paw to bring back her son

- **A** ☐ about a month after his funeral.
- **B** ☐ about a week after his funeral.
- **C** ☐ about two weeks after his funeral.

4 Where was the monkey's paw?

- **A** ☐ In their bedroom.
- **B** ☐ In the kitchen.
- **C** ☐ In the living room.

5 Mrs White wanted the paw

- **A** ☐ so she could wish for Herbert to return.
- **B** ☐ so her husband could make a second wish.
- **C** ☐ so she could destroy it.

2 **Here are some verbs from Part Three that help increase the atmosphere of suspense.**
Look at the sentences below and then match a verb to the correct definition.

- I tried not to make any noise but the kitchen door **creaked** loudly when I opened it.
- I **peered** at the man coming towards me in the fog.
- I knew that they had told her the terrible news because I could hear her **wailing** in the other room.
- When the lights went out, I **groped** about in the drawer for a candle, but I couldn't find one.
- Everybody was asleep so I **crept** up to my bedroom.
- 'Have I really won the lottery?' I **stammered**.

a. to creak
b. to stammer
c. to peer
d. to creep (crept, crept)
e. to wail
f. to grope

1. ☐ To look for something by feeling with your hands.
2. ☐ To speak with pauses and repetitions because of a strong emotion.
3. ☐ To look carefully at something, especially something that is difficult to see.
4. ☐ To move slowly and quietly.
5. ☐ To make a long, acute sound expressing pain or extreme sadness.
6. ☐ To make a sharp sound.

PART THREE

Having buried their son in a huge new cemetery two miles away, the old couple came back to a house full of shadow and silence. It was all over so quickly that at first they hardly realized it; they expected something else to happen, something that would lift the intolerable weight from their old hearts.

But the days passed and their expectation changed to resignation. They hardly talked — they had nothing to talk about now — and their days were long and empty.

It was about a week later that the old man woke up suddenly in the night and heard the sound of quiet crying coming from the window. He sat up and listened.

'Come back to bed,' he said tenderly. 'You'll get cold.'

'It is colder for my son,' said his wife, who continued weeping.

The sound of it gradually faded as the old man fell asleep again, until a sudden wild cry from his wife woke him up with a start.[1]

'The paw!' she cried wildly. 'The monkey's paw!'

1. **with a start** : with a sudden movement.

'Where? Where is it? What's the matter?' the old man said, alarmed.

She came towards him. 'I want it. You haven't destroyed it?'

'It's in the living room,' he replied, amazed. 'Why?'

Mrs White laughed and cried at the same time, and kissed his cheek.[1]

'I've only just thought of it,' she said hysterically. 'Why didn't I think of it before? Why didn't you think of it?'

'Think of what?'

'The other two wishes. We've only had one.'

'Wasn't that enough?' he demanded fiercely.

'No, we'll have one more. Go down and get it quickly and wish our boy alive again.'

The old man sat up in bed and threw the bedclothes from his trembling body.

'Good God, you are mad!' he cried.

'Get it,' his wife said, breathlessly. 'Get it quickly and wish — Oh, my boy, my boy!'

Mr White lit the candle with a match. 'Get back to bed. You don't know what you're saying.'

But the old woman said feverishly, 'Our first wish was granted. Why not the second?'

'A coincidence,' the old man stammered.

'Go and get it and wish.' Mrs White was trembling with excitement.

The old man looked at her and his voice shook. 'He has been dead ten days, and also — I could only recognize him by his

1. **cheek** : part of the face below the eye.

clothes. He was too horrible for you to see then. What do you think he looks like now?'

But his wife pulled him towards the door. 'Bring him back. Do you think I'm frightened of my own son?'

He went downstairs in the darkness, and felt his way to the living room, and then to the mantelpiece. [1] The talisman was there. Suddenly he was possessed by a horrible fear that his unspoken wish might bring his mutilated son back before he could escape from the room. In a cold sweat [2] he groped his way round the table and along the wall until he was in the small passage. The dirty, twisted, dried-up, thing was in his hand.

Even his wife's face seemed different as he entered the bedroom. It was white and expectant, and her expression seemed unnatural. He was afraid of her.

'Wish!' she cried in a strong voice.

'It is foolish and wicked,' he stammered, hesitating.

'Wish!' repeated his wife.

He raised his hand. 'I wish my son alive again.'

The paw fell to the floor. He looked at it in fear. Then he fell trembling into a chair. With burning eyes his wife walked to the window and raised the blind. [3]

Mr White sat until he was chilled to the bone, [4] glancing occasionally at his wife who was peering through the window. The candle-flame, which had burned low, threw pulsating shadows on the ceiling and walls, until it slowly went out. The old man, feeling an

1. **mantelpiece** : structure with a shelf that encloses a fireplace.
2. **sweat** : fluid on the skin, here caused by fear.
3. **blind** : piece of flexible material on the window for keeping out the light.
4. **chilled... bone** : very cold.

inexpressible relief[1] that the wish had not worked, crept back to bed. A few minutes later his wife also came to bed, silent and depressed.

Neither spoke, but lay silently listening to the ticking of the clock. A stair creaked; a squeaky mouse ran noisily through the wall. The darkness was oppressive. After building up his courage for some time, Mr White lit a match and, taking the matchbox with him, went downstairs for a candle.

At the bottom of the stairs the match went out. He paused to strike another one, and at the same moment there was a knock at the door, a knock so quiet it was almost inaudible.

The matches fell from his hand. He stood like a statue, his breath suspended. The knock came again. He turned and fled[2] back to the bedroom, closing the door behind him. A third knock sounded through the house.

'What's that!' shouted the old woman, sitting up suddenly.

'A rat.' Mr White's voice shook. 'A rat. It passed me on the stairs.'

His wife sat listening. A loud knock echoed through the house.

'It's Herbert!' she screamed. 'It's Herbert!'

She ran to the bedroom door, but her husband was faster than her. He caught her by the arm and held her tightly.

'What are you going to do?' he whispered.

Mrs White struggled[3] to free herself. 'It's my boy, it's Herbert! I forgot it was two miles away. What are you holding me for? Let go. I must open the door.'

'For God's sake don't let it in!' cried the old man, trembling.

1. **relief** [re'li:f] : freedom from anxiety.
2. **fled** : (flee, fled, fled) ran quickly in fear.
3. **struggled** : made violent movements.

'You're afraid of your own son. Let me go. I'm coming, Herbert, I'm coming!'

There was another knock, and another. With a sudden violent movement the old woman broke free and ran from the room. Mr White followed her to the top of the stairs and appealed to her to stop as she hurried downstairs. He heard the chain rattle back; [1] the stiff bolt [2] at the bottom of the door was slowly pulled open. Then Mrs White's voice came, strained and breathless:

'The bolt at the top! I can't reach it. Come down!'

But Mr White was on his hands and knees, groping wildly on the floor, trying to find the paw. If he could only find it before the thing outside got in! Now a continuous knocking echoed through the house. He heard the sound of a chair scraping [3] across the passage floor as his wife pulled it against the door. He heard the creaking of the bolt as it was slowly opened, and at the same moment he found the monkey's paw and frantically breathed his third and last wish.

The knocking stopped suddenly, though it still echoed in the house. He heard the chair scraping back from the door; he heard the door open. A cold wind rushed up the stairs and a long, loud wail of disappointment and misery broke from his wife. It gave him the courage to run to her side, then to the gate outside. The street lamp opposite the house shone flickeringly on a quiet and deserted road.

1. **rattle back** : make a metallic noise.
2. **stiff bolt** : long piece of metal used to lock the door.
3. **scraping** : making a hard, unpleasant noise.

Go back to the text

1 Answer the following questions.

a. What was the Whites' life like after the death of their son?

b. How did Mr White try to convince his wife that it would be horrible if their son came back?

c. How did she respond?

d. Why did Mr White become afraid of his wife?

e. Why did Mr White begin to feel relief after he had wished his son alive again?

f. What was the first sign that Herbert had come back?

g. Why did Mr White have enough time to make the third wish before his wife could let Herbert in?

h. What happened after he made the third wish?

2 What was the sequence of fateful events that led to Mr White getting the £200? Put the sentences (a-g opposite) in order and write them in the correct boxes.

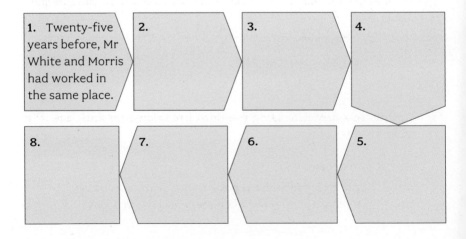

1. Twenty-five years before, Mr White and Morris had worked in the same place.

2.

3.

4.

5.

6.

7.

8.

a. Mr White took the paw from the fire.

b. Morris had told Mr White about the paw a few days before the visit.

c. The Whites hadn't finished paying for their house.

d. Morris joined the army and went to India, where he first got the monkey's paw.

e. Herbert was accidentally killed at work.

f. Mr White was sceptical about the paw but Herbert suggested the £200 solution.

g. When Morris visited the Whites he brought the paw with him.

'If Mr White hadn't made the first wish, Herbert wouldn't have died'

To talk about the consequences of past actions or past situations that did not happen, we use **if** + the **Past Perfect** then **would have** + **the past participle**. This is called the **third conditional**.

Look at these examples:

- If he **had studied** harder, he **would have passed** the exam.
- If I **had missed** that train, I **wouldn't have made** it on time to the airport.
- It **wouldn't have been** such a success if you **hadn't worked** as hard as you did.

3 **Now write a sentence using the third conditional for each event in exercise 2.**

Here is an example:

*If Mr White and Sergeant Morris **hadn't worked** in the same place twenty-five years ago, they **wouldn't have known** each other.*

4 Complete the crossword.

Across

3. He was so afraid, in fact he was .... to the bone.
6. The holy man who made the spell.
7. This fluid forms on the skin if you are afraid or very hot.
8. An object that is believed to have magical powers.
10. If you move very slowly and quietly, you ....
11. This is used to cover windows, but is not a curtain.
13. The object in this story.
14. Entertainers who throw two or more balls in the air, catching and throwing each in succession.
16. A sharp noise that a door can make if it needs oil.
17. Tell someone to do something in a very strong way.

Down

1. Expression used to say that you have won a chess game.
2. Run away from something when very afraid.
4. This structure encloses a fireplace.
5. Herbert .... at the fire for a long time.
6. Make a very sudden movement of surprise.
9. A noise that is made if you move a chair across a hard floor without lifting it.
12. Mr White thinks his path is like this.
13. To try to see something when vision is restricted.
14. Herbert didn't believe the story and thought it was all a joke.
15. Move around in the darkness, touching what is around you to help you.

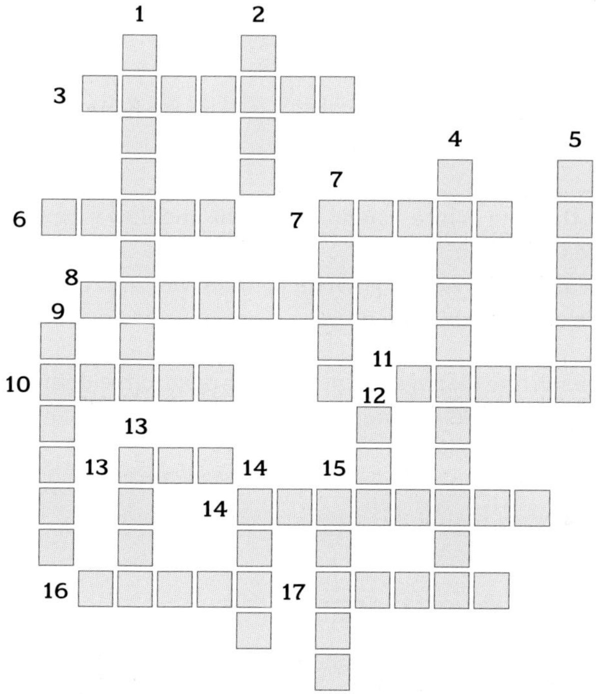

5 **Now answer these questions.**

a. There are two aspects of the game of **chess**:
   1. You can choose to move any piece you want.
   2. You can only move each piece in a particular way, according to the rules.

   Why do you think the author decided to show Mr White and Herbert playing chess at the beginning of the story?

b. The Sergeant Major joined the army and had an exciting, unusual life. But he said to Mr White, 'You're better here where you are.'
   Can you think of any reason(s) why?

c. Although the Whites weren't poor, they didn't have a lot of money. In what way is this important in the story?

d. Mr White took the paw from the fire and kept it. Was this fate or free choice? What were the consequences?

e. Mr White wished for £200, *not* his son's death — but both happened. Was this because of the paw or was it simply coincidence?

FCE **6** **Imagine that Mr White couldn't find the monkey's paw and didn't make the third wish.**
Write an alternative ending. Write your answer in 120-180 words.
You can begin like this:

Finally Mrs White managed to pull a chair next to the door. She reached up and pulled the bolt at the top and the door slowly opened. A gust of cold air blew into the house and...

INTERNET PROJECT

Urban Legends are mysterious and sometimes horrific stories that are set in an urban environment and reported as true. Howevers, can we be sure?
Let's find out about some popular urban legends on the Internet.
Follow these instructions to be directed to the correct Web site.

- Connect to the Internet and go to www.blackcat-cideb.com or www.cideb.it
- Insert the title or part of the title using our search engine.
- Open the page for *Gothic Short Stories.* Click on the project link symbol @
- Go down the page until you find the title of this book and click on the link with the symbol.

With a partner choose one of the urban legends. Tell the class about it. Do you think it could be true?

The PHANTOM COACH

by **Amelia B. Edwards**

Before you read

FCE 1 **A. Read the text below, and think of the word which best fits each space. Use only one word in each space.**

The events I am (**1**) .... to tell you about are true. They happened to me 20 years (**2**) ...., but I remember them (**3**) .... if they happened only yesterday. During those 20 years, I have told only one person about them, and now I find (**4**) .... difficult to overcome a certain reluctance. You see, I don't want you to force your conclusions on me. I believe in the evidence (**5**) .... my own senses and I won't (**6**) .... my mind.

One December day 20 years ago I went out hunting with my gun, (**7**) .... I had no luck all day. The east wind was cold on that wide, empty moor (**8**) .... the north of England. It wasn't a pleasant place in (**9**) .... to lose your way — and I had lost my way. A snowstorm was coming and the evening sky was (**10**) .... dark. I looked anxiously (**11**) .... the distance but I couldn't see (**12**) .... signs of habitation — no fences, no cultivated land. So I walked (**13**) .... , hoping to find shelter somewhere. I (**14**) .... been out since dawn and I was very tired.

5 **B. Now listen to the recording and check your answers.**

C. Now that you have read the beginning of 'The Phantom Coach' can you guess what this story is going to be about?

- A man who is mentally ill
- An unforgettable journey by coach
- A frightening supernatural experience
- Other

PART ONE

1 The events I am going to tell you about are true. They happened to me 20 years ago but I remember them as if they happened only yesterday. During those 20 years I have told only one person about them, and now I find it difficult to overcome a certain reluctance. You see, I don't want you to force your conclusions on me. I believe in the evidence of my own senses and I won't change my mind.

2 One December day 20 years ago I went out hunting with my gun, but I had no luck all day. The east wind was cold on that wide, empty moor [1] in the north of England. It wasn't a pleasant place in which to lose your way — and I had lost my way. A snowstorm was coming and the evening sky was getting dark. I looked anxiously into the distance but I couldn't see any signs of habitation — no fences, [2] no cultivated land. So I walked on, hoping to find shelter [3] somewhere. I had been out since dawn and I was very tired. END

While I was walking the snow began to fall. It grew colder and colder, and then the night came down rapidly. My heart grew

1. **moor** [mɔːr] : high area of wild, uncultivated land.
2. **fences** : barriers of wood or wire around an area of land.
3. **shelter** : protection from the weather, i.e. a building.

heavy as I thought of my young wife watching for me through the window of the little inn. [1] We had been married only four months and we were staying in a remote little village called Dwolding on the edge of the English moors. We were very much in love and very happy. That morning when I left my wife I promised to return before sunset. If only I had kept that promise! But even now I thought that if I could find shelter and a guide I might get back to my wife before midnight.

3 The snow continued to fall and the night got darker. I stopped and shouted now and then, but that seemed to make the silence deeper. I got frightened when I remembered stories of travellers who had fallen asleep in the snow and died. Could I walk all night in the snow? Death! I trembled, thinking how hard it would be for my darling wife if I died. No, no, I couldn't stand the thought of it, so I shouted louder and longer. And then I listened. Did I hear something? Was there an answer to my shouts? Suddenly I saw a speck [2] of light in the darkness and I ran fast towards it. Then to my great joy I found myself face to face with an old man carrying a lantern.

4 'Thank God!' I exclaimed.

'What for?' growled [3] the old man, lifting the lantern and looking into my face.

'Well — for you. I got lost in the snow.'

'People get lost around here now and then — so why shouldn't you?' the old man said rudely.

'Maybe you're right, my friend, but I don't want to be lost without you. How far am I from Dwolding?'

1. **inn** : small pub/hotel (usually in the country).
2. **speck** : very small spot.
3. **growled** : spoke in a deep, guttural way (usually used for dogs).

'Twenty miles, more or less.'

'And the nearest village?'

'That's twelve miles away.'

'Where do you live then?'

'Over that way.'

'Are you going home?'

'Maybe.'

'Then I'm going with you.'

But the old man shook his head. 'It's no good. He won't let you in — not Him.'

'And who is Him?'

'The master.'

'Who is the master?'

'Mind your own business,' was the rude reply.

'All right, friend,' I said. 'You lead the way and I'll follow. I'm sure the master will give me food and shelter tonight.'

'Well, you can only try,' muttered [1] my guide and, shaking his head, he went off through the snow.

Soon I saw the large shape of a house in the darkness.

'Is this the house?' I asked.

'This is it,' said the man, putting a key in the door, which was like the door of a prison.

5 I stood close behind him, ready to enter immediately, and as soon as he turned the key I pushed past him into the house.

I found myself in a great hall with rafters [2] on the ceiling. Hams and dried herbs hung from them. On the floor there were sacks of flour and agricultural tools. To my surprise there was a

1. **muttered** : spoke in a low, indistinct way.
2. **rafters** : long parallel pieces of wood supporting the roof.

large telescope on four wheels in the centre of the hall. While I was examining it a bell rang.

'That's for you,' said my guide. 'His room's over there.'

I went and knocked at a small black door at one end of the hall. Receiving no answer, I entered without permission and saw a huge old man with white hair standing at a table covered with books and papers.

'Who are you?' he said. 'How did you come here? What do you want?'

'James Murray. On foot across the moor. Meat, drink, and sleep.'

The man frowned. [1] 'This is not a hotel. What right have you to force yourself on me?'

'The right of self-preservation. Outside I would be dead in the snow before dawn.'

6 The man looked out of the window. 'Hmm, that's true I suppose. Well, you can stay here until morning.' Then, turning to my guide, he said, 'Jacob, serve the dinner.'

Indicating a seat for me, my host sat down at the table and began to study his books again. I sat near the fire and looked round the room with curiosity. The floor was covered with maps, papers and books. There were cupboards full of geological objects, bottles of chemicals, and other pieces of equipment. A model of the solar system and a microscope stood on a shelf beside me. I stared at my strange surroundings in amazement. Then I turned my attention to the master. He had a fine head, covered with thick white hair, and an expression of deep concentration. He looked like Beethoven the composer.

7 Suddenly the door opened and Jacob brought in the dinner and the master invited me to eat at the table. We ate in silence. When

1. **frowned** : made a facial expression showing displeasure.

we had finished, Jacob took the dishes away and I took my chair back to the fire. To my surprise the master came and sat with me. He told me that he had lived alone for twenty-three years and I was the first stranger he had seen for four years. Then he began to tell me about his life. He had been a student of the supernatural in his youth and had studied hard, learning everything the old philosophers said about spirits, ghosts and spectres.

'But modern science doesn't accept the supernatural,' he continued. 'And because I studied these marvels of the spirit world the scientists said I was crazy.'

The scientists and philosophers had laughed at him and destroyed his work and his reputation. So he had come to live in this remote part of England. He had forgotten the world and the world had forgotten him. It was a sad story. When he had finished speaking he went to the window.

8 'It has stopped snowing,' he said.

I jumped quickly to my feet, ready to go. But then I said in despair, 'No, it's impossible for me to walk twenty miles across the moor. Oh, I'll never see my darling wife tonight!'

'Your wife? Where is she?'

'At Dwolding. Oh, I'd give a thousand pounds now for a horse and guide!'

The master smiled at this. 'You can get to Dwolding for much less than a thousand pounds. The night mail coach from the north goes to Dwolding. It passes a certain crossroads only five miles from here in about an hour and a quarter. Jacob can guide you there.

He rang the bell and gave old Jacob his directions. Then he offered me a glass of whisky, which I drank. It was very strong.

'It will keep out the cold,' said the master. 'Now you must go. Goodnight.'

Go back to the text

FCE **1** **Part One has been divided into eight parts. Choose from the list A-I the heading which best summarizes each part. There is one extra heading which you do not need to use.**

A	☐	What are all these things for?
B	☐	Saved!
C	☐	A cheaper way home
D	☐	No authorization is needed to save a life
E	☐	A promise to keep
F	☐	No escape
G	☐	You don't want me, but I want you
H	☐	Unpopular ideas
I	☐	My eyes and ears don't lie

2 **Are the following statements true (T) or false (F)? Correct the false ones.**

	T	F
a. James Murray has told many people about the event of the story.	☐	☐
b. James Murray became frightened when he realized that he was lost.	☐	☐
c. The old man could not understand how James Murray had got lost.	☐	☐
d. The old man was happy to lead James Murray to his home.	☐	☐
e. James Murray justified his coming uninvited into the house by saying that he would not have survived the night out in the snow.	☐	☐
f. The master's house was full of scientific instruments.	☐	☐
g. The master did not accept the supernatural ideas of the old philosophers.	☐	☐
h. The master told Jacob to take James Murray to Dwolding.	☐	☐

FCE **3** **Complete the second sentence so that it has a similar meaning to the first sentence, using the word given. Do not change the word given. You must use between two and five words, including the word given. There is an example at the beginning (0).**

0 I walked on, hoping to find shelter.
as
I walked on as I hoped to find shelter.

1 Was there an answer to my shouts?
answer
Did .... shouts?

2 'Are you going home?' I asked the old man.
if
I asked the old man .... home.

3 The snow continued to fall.
not
The .... falling.

4 We were very much in love.
each
We .... very much.

5 If only I had kept that promise!
broken
If only .... that promise.

6 Receiving no answer, I entered without permission.
though
I entered without permission .... no answer.

7 We ate in silence.
saying
We ate .... a word.

8 You can get to Dwolding for much less than a thousand pounds.
cost
It .... than a thousand pounds to get to Dwolding.

Before you go on

FCE **1** **Listen to the beginning of Part Two and complete the sentences with a word or a phrase.**

6

1 On the silent moor, James followed Jacob with his ....

2 The words that the master had said about the supernatural had ....

3 Jacob told him to follow .... on his right.

4 James needed to walk about .... to get to the crossroads.

5 The accident had happened near the signpost where .... was broken.

6 About nine years ago .... had had an accident and seven people were killed.

7 The accident had killed .... as well as the coachman, the guard and an outside passenger.

8 As James was walking he tried not to think about ....

T: GRADE 8

2 **Topic — The supernatural**
What do you think about the supernatural? Tell the class your opinions. You can use these questions to help you.

a. Have you ever had a supernatural experience?

b. Do you believe in the supernatural?

c. What do you think of people who say they have seen ghost?

d. Can you think of any rational explanation for a supernatural experience?

e. What do you think you would do if you saw a ghost?

PART TWO

I thanked him for his kind hospitality, and in a minute Jacob and I were out on the white, silent moor. It was freezing cold. No stars shone in the black sky; the only sound was the crunching of the snow under our feet. Jacob walked in front of me and I followed with my gun on my shoulder. I was thinking of the old master. His voice and his words still rang in my ears. What he had said about the supernatural excited my imagination. Then Jacob's voice broke into my thoughts.

'Follow this stone wall on your right and you can't miss the crossroads.'

'How far is it?'

'About three miles. This road is steep [1] and narrow so be careful, especially near the signpost where the stone wall is broken. It hasn't been repaired since the accident.'

'What accident?'

'About nine years ago the night mail coach crashed through

1. **steep** : at an acute angle.

the wall near the signpost and fell into the valley. There were four passengers inside. All of them were killed. The coachman, the guard and an outside passenger died too.'

'How horrible! Near the signpost, you say? I'll remember.'

I gave Jacob some money and he went away into the darkness. Then I began to walk along the road, keeping the stone wall to my right. How silent and lonely it was now! I felt so lonely I started to sing a tune. The night air became colder and colder. My feet were like ice. I walked faster to keep warm and I tried to occupy my mind so that I wouldn't think about the master's talk of the supernatural. END

After a while I had to stop and rest. As I leaned[1] against the stone wall to get my breath back I saw a point of light in the distance. At first I thought it was Jacob coming back, but then I saw a second light exactly like the first and I guessed that a vehicle was approaching. I was surprised. What was a vehicle doing on this steep, dangerous road? But there could be no doubt that it was a carriage coming fast and silently towards me through the thick snow. Was it possible that I had passed the crossroads in the dark and this was the night mail coach I had come to meet?

I didn't have time to answer before the coach came round the bend of the road at full speed. I waved my hat and shouted but the vehicle passed me. Then to my relief the driver stopped and I ran to the coach. The guard seemed to be asleep because he didn't answer my greeting and he didn't move. The passenger sitting next to the coachman didn't even turn his head. I opened

1. **leaned** : supported my body.

the door and looked in. There were three people inside. I got in and sat in a corner, feeling very glad about my good luck.

Inside the coach it seemed, if possible, even colder than outside, and there was a damp and unpleasant smell. I looked at the other travellers, all men. They were silent but didn't seem to be asleep. Each man was sitting back in his corner and seemed to be lost in thought. I tried to start a conversation.

'It's very cold tonight,' I said to the passenger opposite me.

He lifted his head, looked at me, but didn't reply.

'This is real winter weather,' I added.

Although I couldn't see his face very clearly, I saw that his eyes were looking at me. But he didn't say a word.

I was beginning to feel ill. The icy coldness had penetrated to my bones and the strange smell in the coach was making me feel nauseous. Turning to the traveller on my left I asked, 'Do you mind if I open the window?'

He neither spoke nor moved. I asked again and when he didn't answer I pulled the leather strap [1] impatiently to open the window. The strap broke in my hands. It was then that I noticed the thick mildew [2] on the window – years of accumulated mildew! Now I turned my attention to the condition of the coach. Every part of it was falling to pieces. The whole machine was mouldy. [3] The wood was rotting, [4] the floor was nearly breaking away under my feet.

1. **strap** : piece of material once used to open and shut coach windows.
2. **mildew** ['mɪldjuː] : white fungus-like substance.
3. **mouldy** ['məʊldi] : covered with fungus.
4. **rotting** : so old that it was breaking into pieces.

I said to the third passenger, 'This coach is in a terrible condition. It's rotting away. I suppose the regular mail coach is under repair, is it?'

He moved his head slowly and looked at me without saying a word. I will never forget that look as long as I live. It froze my heart

and it freezes my heart now when I remember it. His eyes glowed an unnatural red. His face was as purple as a corpse [1] and his lips were pulled back as if in the agony of death, showing his bright teeth.

1. **corpse** : dead body.

An awful horror came over me. I looked at my opposite neighbour. He was looking at me too with the same red glow in his eyes. I turned to the passenger next to me and saw – oh God, how can I describe it! – I saw that he was dead. All of them were dead! The pale, phosphorescent light of putrefaction played on their faces and their hair, which was damp with the dampness of the grave. Their rotting clothes were dirty with mud and their hands were the hands of long-dead corpses. Only their terrible eyes were living – and those eyes were looking at me menacingly.

With a scream of terror I threw myself at the door and tried to open it. At that moment I saw the moon shining on the signpost, the broken wall, and the black valley below. Then the coach rocked and fell like a ship at sea, there was a tremendous crash, a terrifying sense of falling... for a moment I felt a great pain... and then, darkness.

It seemed years later that I woke up one morning from a deep sleep and found my wife sitting by my bed. She told me I had fallen over a precipice near the crossroads and had only survived death by landing in deep snow. Some men had found me at dawn, carried me to safety, and called a doctor. When the doctor came I was in a state of delirium, and had a broken arm. My name and address were on some letters in my pocket so the doctor was able to contact my wife, who came and nursed me with loving care until I was out of danger.

The place where I fell was, of course, exactly where the night mail coach had crashed nine years before. I have never told my wife about the terrible events of that night. I told the doctor but he thought it was all a dream caused by the fever in my brain. Well, others can form any conclusions they want – I know that 20 years ago I was the fourth passenger inside the Phantom Coach.

Go back to the text

1 Answer the following questions.

- **a.** How many passengers were travelling inside the coach that fell into the valley?
- **b.** Why was James Murray surprised to see a coach arriving?
- **c.** How many passengers were travelling inside the coach that stopped for James Murray?
- **d.** What was the coach like?
- **e.** Why did James Murray begin to feel ill?
- **f.** What were the passengers in the coach like?
- **g.** What did James Murray's wife believe had happened?
- **h.** Where was the place where James Murray fell?

2 Amelia B. Edwards wrote this story in 1864 (see box 5). Can you complete boxes 1, 2 and 3 and part of box 4 on the diagram? Link the information given in the story to the dates.

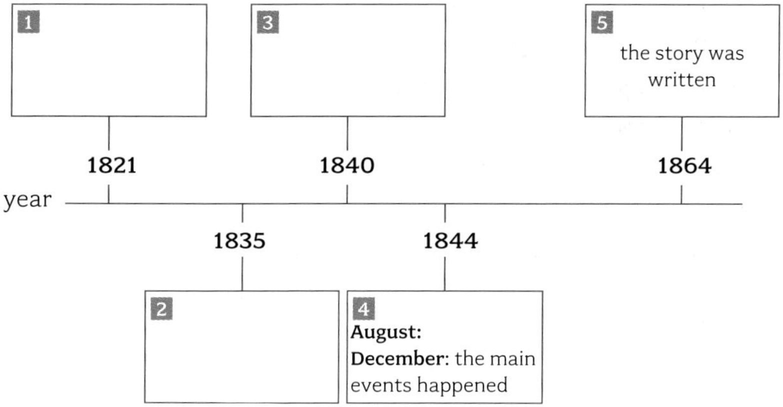

'The strange smell was making me feel nauseous'

Look at these sentences with **make** and **let**. Notice that the infinitive is without **to**.

- The strange smell **made** me **feel** nauseous.
- The policeman **made** him **stop** his car.
- My brother never **lets** me **drive** his car.
- Our teacher **lets** us **use** calculators during exams.

3 Write complete sentences using the words given and *let* or *make*. Use an appropriate tense according to the context.

Examples: That film/me/cry
That film made me cry.
Jane/stay/in her apartment/while she is away
Jane is going to let me stay in her apartment while she is away.

a. Wine/me/feel sleepy

....

b. You/me/sleep/on your sofa/tonight?

....

c. My parents/me/go to the party/if I finish my homework

....

d. 'I/you/go/, if you tell me the name of the other criminals,' said the policeman

....

e. The policeman/them/move their car

....

f. Red roses/always/me/think of my boyfriend in Paris

....

g. I am sorry but I/can't/you/come in/if you don't have a ticket

....

I believe in the evidence of my senses

FCE **4** **Pretend that you are the doctor who treated James Murray; you do not believe his story. Write a short report explaining why he had those strange hallucinations. Include the following information:**

- how he got lost
- why he was particularly anxious
- who saved him
- how he really fell
- how James Murray believes he fell

5 **During the narrative James Murray feels the emotions and sensations below. Write sentences explaining why.**

1. On the moor

a. anxious : ....

b. tired : ....

c. frightened : ....

d. joyful : ....

2. In the coach

a. glad : ....

b. nauseous : ....

c. impatient : ....

d. horror : ....

e. pain : ....

6 **Complete this summary of the story with the phrases from the box below. Remember to put the words of each phrase in the correct order.**

coach mail night	a with man lantern old	to falling pieces
inside passengers three	was snowstorm coming	
been accident an had	way had his lost	out the jump coach of
a coming saw coach	of supernatural the student	
the passengers inside four	life his story of	
moved neither nor spoke	he when up woke	
the been fourth had passenger	to Dwolding return	
were the passengers dead	quarter a hour and	

One cold day in December James Murray [1]................................ on the moors. The weather was cold and a [2]................................ . James shouted for help but nobody came. Then he saw an [3]................................, who took him to a large house. There James met 'the master'. This man had been a [4]................................ and knew everything about it. He told James the [5]................................ .

When it had stopped snowing James wanted to [6]................................ but he realized it was impossible. Then the master explained that there was a [7]................................ that passed a crossroads five miles away in an [8]................................ . So James decided to take it. On the way to the crossroads Jacob told him that nine years before there [9]................................ near a signpost. The night coach had crashed into the valley and [10]................................ had died. Alone, James walked on, trying not to think about the supernatural. Then, while he was resting, he [11]................................ along the road.

When it pulled up he got in. There were [12]................................ . James tried to speak to them but they [13]................................ . Then he noticed that the coach was mouldy and [14]................................ . The next moment he realized that all [15]................................; only their eyes were alive — and they were looking at him menacingly! With a scream James tried to [16]................................, which fell into the valley below.

[17]................................ his wife was sitting by his bed. She said he had fallen over a precipice, but James knew that he [18]................................ inside the Phantom Coach.

The Gothic *Craze*[1]

During the last part of the eighteenth century, French culture had a strong influence on England. France could boast[2] the most sophisticated and opulent court of all of Europe, as well as that brilliant group of thinkers known as the philosophes, which included Diderot, Voltaire, Rousseau, Condorcet and Helvétius. Indeed many English liberal thinkers agreed with their beliefs about rationalism in religion and a rational reform of society.

So, it is strange that in England a taste[3] emerged that was the complete opposite of the French Enlightenment, the Gothic dark. What is even stranger, Horace Walpole, the man who began the Gothic craze in literature and architecture was an admirer of French culture. Walpole (the son of Britain's first prime minister, Robert Walpole) was an important literary man and art connoisseur. He restructured Strawberry Hill, his house on the river Thames, to imitate Gothic architecture.

For Horace Walpole, the word 'Gothic' was nearly synonymous with the Dark Ages, i.e., the Middle Ages, or, in other words, a primitive and wild period of dark churches and castles surrounded by clouds of mystery.

1. **craze** : something that is very popular for a short time.
2. **boast** : be proud of.
3. **taste** : (here) style.

View of Strawberry Hill, Middlesex from the gardens (19th century) by Gustave E. Sintzenich.

Walpole said that *The Castle of Otranto* (1764), the book that started the Gothic craze, was inspired by a dream: 'I thought myself in an ancient castle... and that on the upper banister [1] of the staircase I saw a gigantic hand in armour.' This novel features ghosts, giants, castles and statues that come to life, and more importantly its characters give unrestrained vent [2] to their emotions.

The Castle of Otranto was a huge success: a second edition was published within a year and ten more editions shortly followed. The Gothic craze had begun and would last until the 1820s.

1. **banister** : piece of wood at the side of a staircase that you use to hold on to.
2. **unrestrained vent** : unreserved expression.

Gothic novels were generally set in Medieval times, often in Italy, and described haunted houses and castles, dungeons, secret passageways, flashes of lightning, screams, bloody hands, ghosts, graveyards, corpses coming to life and extreme passions of all sorts. What is more, as the literary critic Walter Allen noted, Gothic novels were often characterized by 'a peculiarly intense relationship between the characters and their immediate environments. Character and environment is, as it were, humanized; and the character himself is as he is because of the environment and cannot be detached from it; it is a necessary element for his existence, a special kind of air.'

View of Corfe Castle by Matthew Antrobus.

Another important writer of Gothic novels was Mrs Ann Radcliffe, a shy woman who rarely left her homes in London and Bath. She was, however, an expert at describing exotic places and the wild forces of nature. Her most famous novel, *The Mysteries of Udolpho* (1794), is set in a gloomy castle in Italy where the heroine is taken prisoner by her evil uncle.

The period of the Gothic craze ended with two of its finest novels. The first, *Frankenstein* (1818) by Mary Shelley is a fine work of art

Boris Karloff as the monster in the 1932 film version of **Frankenstein** directed by James Whale.

whose Gothic hero, Dr Victor Frankenstein, is obsessed with creating life.

The other work was Charles Maturin's *Melmouth the Wanderer* (1820). Melmouth, the main character of the novel, is over one hundred years old. He has sold his soul to the devil for a prolonged life. This long life, though, causes him to suffer atrociously, and he can only escape his agony by persuading someone else to take over his part.

Even though the craze for Gothic literature ended in the early 1820s, it continued to influence many writers after this time. Gothic elements can be found in the books of Charles Dickens, the Brontë sisters, Edgar Allan Poe, Nathaniel Hawthorne and some important modern writers such as Henry James and William Faulkner.

Also, Gothic literature in the strict sense has continued. For example, one of Gothic literature's masterpieces Bram Stoker's *Dracula* was published in 1897, and contemporary writers such as Ann Rice, the author of the Vampire Chronicles, and Stephen King have had enormous success.

Finally, we should note that all the conventions of Gothic literature have entered the language of films. What filmgoer does not know what a creaking door in an old abandoned house during a thunder storm means (even if the house is located in the suburbs of America)? In short, the Gothic craze continues.

1 **Answer the following questions.**

a. What did the word 'Gothic' mean for Horace Walpole?

b. What were some of the common elements of Gothic novels?

c. When did the Gothic craze begin?

d. According to the critic Walter Allen, in Gothic novels what is often the relationship between characters and their environment?

e. What was Dr Frankenstein's obsession?

f. Which contemporary writers have written successful Gothic novels?

g. Why can we say that in a certain sense the Gothic craze continues to this day?

INTERNET PROJECT

Let's find out some more about authors of Gothic stories.
Follow these instructions to be directed to the correct Web site.

- Connect to the Internet and go to www.blackcat-cideb.com or www.cideb.it
- Insert the title or part of the title using our search engine.
- Open the page for *Gothic Short Stories*. Click on the project link symbol @
- Go down the page until you find the title of this book and click on the link with the symbol.

With a partner choose one of the authors and prepare a brief biography on them. Include information about their life and their most famous works.

The Fall of the HOUSE OF USHER

by **Edgar Allan Poe**

Before you read

1 Describing Horror

Here are some adjectives from Part One. Match them to the correct definition. Use the sentences below to help you.

- When I looked at the ***grim*** teeth of the angry dog I wanted to run away.
- As I was walking down a dark street, I saw the ***ghastly*** glow of a candle in an old, abandoned house.
- The heat and humidity were so ***oppressive*** that we stayed in our air-conditioned hotel-room until evening.
- The weather has been quite ***melancholy*** since you left — nothing but rain and fog.
- Harry sat by himself in his room with a ***sullen*** look on his face because Mum had told him that he could not go to the football match.

a. oppressive **b.** melancholy **c.** ghastly
d. grim **e.** sullen

1. ☐ Severe and unrelenting in a way that makes you lose your courage.
2. ☐ Very pale or white in a way that makes you think of death or a ghost.
3. ☐ Sad. (Other synonyms of this word which appear in this story are dreary and gloomy.)
4. ☐ Difficult to tolerate or bear.
5. ☐ Hostilely or angrily silent.

2 **Look at the picture of the House of Usher on page 71 and talk about it. Use these questions to help you. You may want to use some of the words from the previous activity.**

a. What is the house like?

b. What impression does it give you?

c. What impression does its setting give you?

d. What type of person would you expect to live in such a house?

e. How would you feel if you had to live there?

FCE **3** **Listen to the beginning of Part One and complete the sentences with a word or a phrase.**

7

1 The story takes place on a ....

2 The narrator feels that the scene of the house surrounded by dead trees was not at all ....

3 Roderick Usher had been one of the narrator's ....

4 Roderick Usher considered the narrator his only ....

5 The Usher family was famous for its charity and its ....

6 For centuries the patrimony of the Usher family had ....

7 Even though no portion of the house had fallen, many individual stones ....

8 In Usher's studio there were many pieces of comfortless furniture along with many ....

PART ONE

I rode on a horse one dull, dark and soundless day in autumn until I came to the melancholy House of Usher. I do not know why but I felt an intolerable gloom. I say intolerable because there was nothing poetic or beautiful about this scene, only the dreary house on the edge of a cliff [1] over a black lake surrounded by dead and rotting trees.

Still, I was planning to spend some weeks here. Its owner, Roderick Usher, had been one of my closest childhood friends even though I had not seen him for many years. However, he had sent me a letter. He wrote me of a mental disease that oppressed him and a great desire to see me, his only personal friend. He hoped that my company would make him feel better. So, I had to come.

Although, we had been very close as boys, I knew very little about my friend because he was so reserved. I knew, however, that he came from a very ancient family famous for both its wonderful works of art and its great acts of charity.

1. **cliff** : high piece of land with a very steep side usually by the sea.

I had also learned too, a very remarkable fact, that the entire Usher family lay in the direct line of descent. [1] So it was that for centuries the patrimony of the family had been handed down from father to son, and that the peasants of that region called both the family itself and the family mansion the 'House of Usher'.

The house itself was incredibly old and it was greatly discoloured by time. Strangely, even though individual stones were ruined and crumbling, [2] no portion of the house had fallen. In fact, the building did not look unstable. However, if you looked very carefully you could see a very thin crack; it ran from the roof of the building in front and made its way down the wall in a zigzag direction until it became lost in the dark waters of the lake.

After observing these things, I rode over a short causeway [3] to the house. A servant took my horse, and a valet led me to the studio of his master through many dark and intricate passages. I felt an increasing gloom as we walked. On one of the staircases, I met the doctor of the family. I thought he looked both cunning [4] and perplexed. He stopped to speak with me a moment and then went on.

Finally the valet opened the door of the studio. It was very large and high. There were many pieces of furniture, but they were all comfortless, antique and tattered. [5] Many books and

1. **direct... descent** : each generation had had a male child who had inherited the house.
2. **crumbling** : breaking into small pieces.
3. **causeway** : raised road or path which goes across wet ground or water.
4. **cunning** : clever but in a dishonest way.
5. **tattered** : torn, ruined.

musical instruments lay about the room too. An air of deep and hopeless gloom hung over and pervaded all.

END

When I came in, Roderick Usher got up from a sofa, and greeted me warmly. We then sat down, and for some moments, while he did not speak, I looked at him with pity and fear. Surely, no man had ever changed in so short a period as had Roderick Usher! I could hardly believe that he was the same person who had been my boyhood friend. The ghastly pallor [1] of his skin and the miraculous shine of his eyes shocked me and even frightened me. His hair, which he had allowed to grow, floated rather than fell about his face.

My friend's actions were incoherent and inconsistent: at times he was full of great energy and at times he was sullen. In this way he spoke about his great desire to see me and his disease. He said that it was a constitutional and family evil, and that he did not think he would find a cure. He suffered from an extreme acuteness of the senses. He could only endure the most insipid food; he could wear only clothing of an certain texture; the odours of all flowers were oppressive; his eyes were tortured by even a faint light; and there were only a few special sounds (and these from stringed instruments) which did not inspire him with horror.

He was also completely dependent on an unusual kind of terror. 'I will perish and die,' he said, 'I must perish in this horrible madness. I am not afraid of danger but I am afraid of its effect — terror. I feel that sooner or later I must abandon life and reason together in this battle with the grim phantasm, FEAR.'

1. **pallor** ['pɑlər] : paleness, whiteness.

He also believed that the gloomy house itself and the dark lake had a great effect on his existence.

He admitted, however, that much of his sadness came from the long illness and the approaching death of his beloved sister — his only companion for many years and his last and only relative on earth. 'Her death,' he said, 'would make me the last of the ancient race of the Ushers.' While he spoke, his sister, the lady Madeline, walked slowly through the other end of the studio, and, without seeing me, disappeared.

None of Madeline's doctors had been able to help her. She suffered from apathy, a gradual wasting away of her person and frequent attacks of catalepsy. [1] Until then she had fought the disease, but that evening she finally gave up, and I learned that the glimpse [2] I had of her would probably be my last — that the lady, at least while living, would be seen by me no more.

For the next few days we did not mention her name, and during this time I tried to make my friend feel better. We painted and read together; or I listened, as if in a dream, to the wild improvisations of his playing the guitar.

One of his paintings was particularly striking. It presented the interior of an immensely long and rectangular tunnel with low walls that were smooth, white and without decoration. You could see that it was far below the earth. It had no window, nor any other light. Still, the whole was full of a ghastly and inappropriate splendour.

He also told me his strange belief that not only did plants have feelings but also inorganic things as well. He believed that

1. **catalepsy** : medical condition where a person may become unconscious or may remain rigid for a long time.
2. **glimpse** : quick look.

the home of his ancestors was somehow alive. The result of this could be seen in the silent, persistent and terrible influence which for centuries had shaped the destinies of his family and which made him what I now saw.

One evening Usher told me that Madeline had died. He was going to keep her body in a family vault [1] for two weeks before burying her in the family cemetery. He had decided to do this because of the strange nature of his sister's disease, his distrust of her doctors and the great distance of the cemetery.

So, I helped Usher with this temporary burial of his sister in the family vault, which was deep underground, directly below my bedroom. In feudal times this vault had been a dungeon and later it was used as a deposit for gunpowder. [2]

When we had placed the coffin [3] in the vault, we lifted up the lid [4] to look at her face. The first thing I noticed was the great similarity between the brother and sister. Usher, guessing my thoughts, told me that he and the deceased had been twins, and that there had always been a strange understanding between them.

Still, we could not look at her for long without fear. This woman who had died so young still had a faint colour, and a strange smile which is so terrible in death; this is not unusual for those who have died of some form of catalepsy. So, we put back the lid of the coffin and returned to our rooms above.

1. **vault** : protected room under a house or in a building.
2. **gunpowder** : explosive substance used in bombs.
3. **coffin** : wooden box where a dead body is placed.
4. **lid** : cover.

Go back to the text

FCE **1 Choose the best answer A, B, C or D.**

1 The narrator went to see Roderick Usher because

A ☐ he was interested in seeing the great artistic creations of the Usher family.

B ☐ he hoped Usher would make him feel better.

C ☐ Usher hoped that the narrator's visit would make him feel better.

D ☐ he was interested in the mental disease that oppressed Usher.

2 What was extraordinary about the house?

A ☐ It was old and discoloured.

B ☐ It looked stable despite the crack in front and the crumbling stones.

C ☐ It was located in such an dreary place.

D ☐ It had been the family home of the Usher family for such a long time.

3 What was the principal symptom of Usher's disease?

A ☐ His eyes had a strange shine.

B ☐ His skin had become very pale.

C ☐ His sense of touch, sight, sound and hearing had become incredibly sensitive.

D ☐ He had a feeling of great fear combined with a desire to be with friends.

4 How did Usher think that he would die?

A ☐ His sister would kill him.

B ☐ From his disease as it got worse.

C ☐ From a fear of danger.

D ☐ From some supernatural cause.

5 What was the nature of Madeline's disease?

A ☐ At times she was full of energy and at other times she was paralysed by fear.
B ☐ She was not interested in doing anything, and at times she fell into a kind of a deep trance.
C ☐ She was oppressed by a deep depression.
D ☐ She could not stand bright lights or loud sounds.

6 Usher thought that the house had feelings and could perceive things because

A ☐ it had strongly influenced the lives of his family for generations.
B ☐ it often made strange noises in the night during storms.
C ☐ it was so large and ugly.
D ☐ the fissure in the front was becoming wider.

7 There had been a great understanding between Usher and his sister because

A ☐ they both suffered from the same disease.
B ☐ they were twins.
C ☐ they spent so much time together.
D ☐ they were both excellent artists.

8 The narrator did not think that the colour that Madeleine retained was strange because

A ☐ she had only been dead for a short time.
B ☐ the coldness of the house preserved her well.
C ☐ a delicate colour on the skin is common in people who die of her disease.
D ☐ she had died very suddenly.

'That evening she finally gave up'

Look at these sentences using **phrasal verbs** with **give**:

- Edgar: Have you solved the mystery yet?
  George: No, but I won't **give up** until I have.
- My mother has a lot of clothes she never wears. I think she should **give** them **away** to the poor.
- The teacher **gave out** the test papers to the students.
- After walking for ten hours, my legs **gave out** and I had to rest for an hour or so.
- Remember to **give** me **back** my pen when you have finished using it.

2 Match the phrasal verbs to the correct definitions below. Notice that *give out* has two different definitions.

☐ **a.** give up
☐ **b.** give away
☐ ☐ **c.** give out
☐ **d.** give back

1. return something to its original owner
2. stop working, to fail
3. stop trying to do something
4. give something to somebody without asking for money
5. distribute

3 Complete the sentences with the correct phrasal verb. Make sure the verb is in the correct tense.

a. I am not going to lend you my English grammar book because you never .... anything ....

b. It looked like our team were going to lose. There were only ten minutes left in the game. But we didn't ...., and in the end we won.

c. During the board meeting the president of the company .... some interesting reports to the board members.

d. Philip: Well, how much money are you going to give me for my car?

Julia: You want money for that old, broken down car?

Philip: Yes, of course. Did you think that I was going to .... it .... ?

e. In the end the engine of the boat ...., and the boat stopped in the middle of the lake.

4 What did Madeleine give up doing?

Before you go on

FCE **1 Listen to the beginning of Part Two, and decide if the following statements are true (T) or false (F).**

8

	T	F
a. After his sister's death Usher read, painted and played music more than before.		
b. He became even paler than before.		
c. Usher's strange behaviour affected the narrator.		
d. The narrator wanted Usher to look at the whirlwind and vapour.		
e. While the narrator was reading a book to his friend he heard a sound somewhere in the house like the sound described in the book.		
f. The book describes how a dragon is killed.		

PART TWO

Several days later I began to see a great change in my friend. He no longer read, painted or played music. He wandered around[1] the mansion and his pallor increased. His voice shook when he spoke, as if from extreme terror. At times I thought that my friend was fighting to tell me some oppressive secret. Other times I thought that he was just mad because he stared into space for hours, as if he were listening to some imaginary sound. It is no wonder that his condition terrified — that it infected me. Slowly I myself began to believe his fantastic superstitions.

Then on the seventh or eighth night after placing Madeline in the vault I felt the full power of these feelings. It was stormy outside and I could not sleep. I tried to convince myself that my feelings came from the gloomy furniture of the room in the dark. Then, for some strange reason, I began to pay attention to some low and indistinct sounds. I could not stand it any more and began to walk back and forth in my room. A few minutes later

1. **wandered around** : moved around slowly without going to anywhere in particular.

Usher entered my room holding a lamp. He was as pale as usual, but now there was a kind of mad laughter in his eyes.

'And haven't you seen it?' he said suddenly, after having stared at me for a few moments in silence. 'You have not seen it? — but wait! You will.' Then he hurried to one of the windows and opened it to the storm outside.

The wind entered the room and nearly lifted us from our feet. It was a windy night of singular terror and beauty. A kind of whirlwind [1] blew around the house, and a heavy vapour blocked out all light from the stars, but all around us was the unnatural and faint glow of that vapour.

'You must not — you will not look at this,' I said to Usher, and I led him with gentle violence from the window to a seat. I then explained to him that the strange light outside was just an electrical phenomenon or perhaps it came from the rotting plants in the lake. So, I picked up a book, 'Mad Trist' by Sir Launcelot Canning, [2] and began to read it to Usher. I hoped that this would bring him some relief.

I then came to that well-known part of the story where Ethelred, the hero of the story, tries to break into the home of the evil hermit. Here the story goes like this:

'And now the courageous Ethelred began to break down the door with his stick. As he hit the door, the wood cracked apart and the sound could be heard throughout the forest.'

1. **whirlwind** : strong wind.
2. **Mad Trist... Canning** : fictional novel created by Poe.

At the end of this sentence I started[1] because I thought that I heard from some remote part of the mansion a sound just like the sound described in the book. Perhaps, though, it was just the sound of the wind, and so I continued the story:

'But Ethelred, when he finally entered, did not see the evil hermit. Instead, he saw a giant dragon with a fiery tongue that was a guarding a palace of gold with a silver floor. On the wall a shield[2] hung on which was written –

'Whoever enters here, a conqueror has been;
Whoever kills the dragon, the shield will win;

'And Ethelred lifted his stick and struck the head of the dragon, which died with such a horrible shriek that Ethelred had to cover his ears. Indeed, such a dreadful noise had never been heard before.'

Here again I stopped suddenly. I was now certain that I heard somewhere in the mansion the exact same shriek described by the novelist. However, I remained calm because I did not want to frighten my friend. I was not at all certain that he had heard those sounds. He had, though, moved his chair so that he faced the door of the room and now his body rocked slowly side to side. I continued the story:

1. **started** : made a sudden movement because surprised.
2. **shield** : curved piece of metal or wood used by soldiers as protection.

'And now Ethelred, having killed the dragon went to get the shield on the wall. But before he even put his hand on the shield, it fell with a terrible ringing sound.'

END

As soon as I had said these words, I heard the same ringing and metallic sound in the house. Completely unnerved, I jumped to my feet, but Usher continued rocking gently in his chair. I rushed to the chair, and he stared in front of him. I put my hand on his shoulder and his whole body shook, and there was a horrible smile on his face. He spoke quickly and indistinctly. I bent over him and finally understood what he was saying:

'Don't you hear it? – yes, I hear it and have heard it. Long – long – long – many minutes, many hours, many days I have heard it, and yet I didn't dare to speak! We have put her living in the tomb! Didn't I tell you that my senses were acute? I now tell you that I heard her moving in the coffin. I heard it many, many days ago – yet I dared not – I dared not speak! And now – tonight – Ethelred – ha! Ha!, the breaking of the hermit's door, and the death-cry of the dragon and the ringing sound of the shield! No we didn't hear those things! We heard, the opening of the coffin, the sound of the doors of her prison and her fighting to escape from the vault! Where can I escape to? Won't she be here soon? Isn't she hurrying here to scream at me for having buried her too soon? Have I not heard her coming up the stairs? Can't I hear the horrible beating of her heart? MADMAN!' At this point he jumped up and shrieked – 'MADMAN! I TELL YOU THAT SHE NOW STANDS OUTSIDE THE DOOR!'

As if the superhuman energy of his words was magical, the door opened. It was the wind that did this, but then outside the door there DID stand Lady Madeline of Usher. There was blood

on her white clothing and signs of the terrible struggle to escape from the coffin on her thin body. For a moment she stood trembling and then, in her violent and now final death-agonies, fell heavily on her brother, pulling him to the floor. In that moment he too died, a victim of the terrors he had anticipated.

I ran from the room terrified. The storm was still blowing with all its force and I crossed the old causeway. Suddenly there was a flash of wild light. I turned around to see where it came from – because behind me there was only the mansion and darkness. The light was of the full and blood-red moon which now shone vividly through that zigzag crack in the house which I described before. While I watched, this crack widened rapidly and then the wind suddenly blew fiercely and the entire moon suddenly appeared. I was amazed as I saw the mighty walls fall apart. Then there was a loud shouting sound like the voice of a thousand waters, and the deep lake below me closed sullenly and silently over the fragments of the 'HOUSE OF USHER'.

Go back to the text

1 **Answer the following questions.**

a. What was strange about the storm?

b. How was Roderick Usher different when he entered the narrator's room?

c. What was the book about that the narrator read to Usher?

d. What three things did the narrator hear while he was reading the story?

e. How did Roderick Usher die?

f. Did Roderick Usher die in the way that he had thought he would die? Explain.

g. What was the flash of wild light that the narrator saw after he had left the mansion?

h. What was the end of the House of Usher?

2 **The Storm**

a. How did the narrator explain the strange storm?

....

b. How do you think Roderick Usher explained it?

....

3 **American Romance**

Edgar Allan Poe is generally considered an American Romantic writer. Typically, the English Romantic poets praised nature and solitude. In England, though, truly wild empty land did not exist, and each person had a distinct and well-established role in society.

However, the America of the early 1800s was still mostly a wild and empty land with no long-established society: there, solitude often had no end, and nature was hostile. Edgar Allan Poe was one of the first important writers to describe this new world.

How is the situation of America of the 1800s reflected in 'The Fall of the House of Usher'? Choose the best answer from below and discuss with a partner.

a. Roderick Usher and Madeleine Usher come from a family that has produced many great works of art and music.

b. Roderick Usher believes that the house itself has made him and his family what they are.

c. The narrator has to ride a long way to find his friend, the last representative of an old family, who has no other companions than his art, his 'living' house and his dying sister.

d. Because of his strange disease, Roderick Usher is only able to tolerate certain kinds of food and music.

Buried Alive

FCE **4** **Read the text about being buried alive, and decide which answer A, B, C or D best fits each space.**

(**0**) Besides.. being a great short-story writer and poet, Edgar Allan Poe was also an excellent magazine editor. He often (**1**) .... in guessing what subjects would interest the general reading public, and one of these subjects was premature burials. Indeed, throughout the 1800s there was a (**2**) .... of public hysteria created by the fear of being buried alive. There were even some (**3**) .... invented so that somebody buried alive by accident could let people know that he was still alive.
We should remember that in the early years of modern medicine, people in comatose (**4**) .... often seemed to be dead. The famous scientist and physician Thomas Henry Huxley (1825-95), wrote that, it was very difficult for ordinary people to tell if someone was dead or in a coma, and that only those doctors with (**5**) .... experience could decide if a person was really dead or not.

Poe himself exploited this (**6**) .... in several of his most famous stories, 'The Cask of Amontillado', 'The Premature Burial', 'The Black

Cat' and 'The Fall of the House of Usher'. Of course, being buried alive (**7**) .... terrifies us today because, as Poe himself wrote, 'We know of nothing so agonising upon Earth — we can (**8**) .... of nothing so hideous in the realms of the nethermost Hell.'

0	**A** Besides	**B** Also	**C** Too	**D** Moreover
1	**A** managed	**B** succeeded	**C** accomplished	**D** could
2	**A** style	**B** kind	**C** group	**D** manner
3	**A** items	**B** objects	**C** utensils	**D** devices
4	**A** states	**B** conditions	**C** ways	**D** situations
5	**A** big	**B** exceedingly	**C** very	**D** great
6	**A** fear	**B** fright	**C** terror	**D** scare
7	**A** still	**B** yet	**C** ever	**D** now
8	**A** imagine	**B** see	**C** dream	**D** picture

FCE **5** **Read the account of an actual premature burial from Poe's short story 'The Premature Burial'.**
Four paragraphs have been removed from the text. Choose from the paragraphs (A-E) the one which fits each gap (1-4). There is one extra paragraph which you do not need to use.

Victorine Lafourcade, a young lady of an illustrious family, was in love with a journalist named Julien Bossuet. Unfortunately it was impossible for her to marry such a poor man, so she married a banker named Monsieur Renelle.

1 ....

She was not buried in the family vault but in an ordinary grave in the village where she was born.

Later, hearing of his lover's death, Julien Bossuet travelled from Paris to the remote village. He wished to dig up her coffin and cut off some of her hair.

2 ....

He then revived her totally with his caresses, and took her quickly to his room in the village. Slowly she acquired her full health again.

3 ....

Twenty years later, the two lovers returned to France. Since she had changed so much in twenty years they felt certain that nobody would recognize her.

4 ....

In the end, the judge said that she did not have to return to her legal husband. He said that the strange circumstances, along with the many years that had gone by, had ended not only equitably but legally the authority of the husband.

A He arrived at her grave at midnight and dug up the coffin. He opened it up and was about to cut of a strand of her hair when he was stopped by the unclosing of her eyes.

B After this, of course, she did not return to her husband. Instead, she fled with her lover to America.

C After their marriage, though, Monsieur Renelle treated her very badly, and after some terrible years with him she died, or at least her condition so closely resembled death as to deceive everyone who saw her.

D After entering the family vault, he had a strange feeling. He felt certain that his lover was alive. So, he rushed to her coffin.

E They were wrong, though, and Monsieur Renelle recognized her the first time he saw her. Indeed, he went before a judge demanding to have his wife back. Mademoiselle Lafourcade, of course, did not wish to return to her husband.

The JUDGE'S HOUSE

by **Bram Stoker**

Before you read

1 These questions are connected to the story you are going to read. Tick one or more of the boxes.

1. When you think of a judge what kind of person do you imagine?
   - a. ☐ severe and grim
   - b. ☐ kind and friendly
   - c. ☐ fair and open-minded
   - d. ☐ detached and calm
   - e. ☐ arrogant and cruel

2. What kind of house would a judge probably live in?
   - a. ☐ a small, modest flat
   - b. ☐ a large, old, expensive flat which needs renovating
   - c. ☐ a dark, depressing cottage
   - d. ☐ a large mansion with antique furniture
   - e. ☐ a quiet suburban villa

3. The main character is a student of mathematics. What kind of person would you expect to meet?
   - a. ☐ rational and logical
   - b. ☐ artistic and impulsive
   - c. ☐ ignorant and lazy
   - d. ☐ tidy and hard-working
   - e. ☐ studious and absent-minded

4. When the story was written in the 1890s, capital punishment existed in England. Do you know which method was used?
   - a. ☐ the guillotine
   - b. ☐ the electric chair
   - c. ☐ a firing squad
   - d. ☐ hanging
   - e. ☐ the gas chamber

5. Which of these animals do you usually associate with cruelty?
   a. ☐ rabbit
   b. ☐ cat
   c. ☐ chicken
   d. ☐ rat
   e. ☐ dove
   f. ☐ falcon

6. This is a horror story which takes place in a judge's house. The author probably decided to choose a judge and not another profession because a judge
   a. ☐ is connected with criminals.
   b. ☐ is an important person in society.
   c. ☐ often frightens people.
   d. ☐ may have the power to sentence people to death.

7. Most of the events in the story happen between midnight and dawn. This is probably because
   a. ☐ that's usually when strange things happen.
   b. ☐ it's dark and quiet.
   c. ☐ it's the coldest part of the night.
   d. ☐ there are ghosts around.

FCE 2 **Listen to the beginning of Part One and complete the sentences with a word or a phrase.**

9

1 Malcolm Malcolmson had to study for an ....

2 It took him .... to get to the town of Benchurch.

3 Benchurch was crowded once every...................... .

4 Mr Carnford, the house agent, told Malcolm that people had an .... about the house.

5 Malcolm paid .... rent.

6 The house where Malcolm was going to stay had belonged to a judge .... ago.

PART ONE

Malcolm Malcolmson was going to take an examination in mathematics very soon so he made up his mind [1] to go somewhere quiet and study by himself. As he wanted to avoid the attractions of the seaside and the countryside he decided to find some quiet little town where there would be nothing to distract him. So, he packed a suitcase with clothes and books and then bought a ticket for the first name on the local timetable which he didn't know.

The journey to Benchurch took three hours. It was a sleepy little town with one inn called The Good Traveller. He went directly there and booked a room for the night. He felt satisfied that nobody knew where he was; he would be able to study in peace. Benchurch was a market town which was crowded only once in three weeks; for the rest of the time it was as quiet as a desert.

The day after his arrival Malcolmson looked for an even quieter place than The Good Traveller. The only house he liked was so quiet and isolated it seemed almost desolate. This was an

1. **made up his mind** : decided.

old, rambling [1] Jacobean [2] house with heavy gables [3] and small windows, surrounded by a massive, high brick wall. In fact, it looked like a fortified house.

'Ah! This is what I've been looking for,' said Malcolmson happily. And he was even happier when he discovered that the place was empty.

He found the house agent, a Mr Carnford, and asked if it was possible to rent the house. The agent seemed very pleased that somebody wanted to live there.

'To tell you the truth,' he said, 'I would let you live there rent-free if the owners agreed. The house has been empty so long that people have some kind of absurd prejudice about it.'

Malcolmson didn't ask the agent what this 'absurd prejudice' was, knowing he would get more information, if he wanted, from other people. So he paid three months' rent, asked for the name of the woman who would cook and clean for him, and went away with the keys in his pocket.

The kind and cheerful landlady of The Good Traveller advised him what provisions food and drink he should buy. But when he told her where he was going to live she turned pale.

'Not the Judge's House!' she said in amazement.

'Why? What's wrong with the place?'

She told him that many years before — perhaps a hundred years or more — the house had belonged to a judge who terrified everyone because of the severe sentences and cruelty of his trials. The landlady couldn't say what exactly was wrong with the house but there was something.

END

1. **rambling** : extending over a large area in an irregular way.
2. **Jacobean** : built during the reign of King James I (1603-25).
3. **gables** : triangular-shaped parts of the roof of a house.

'I wouldn't stay in that house an hour, not even if you paid me,' she said. 'If you'll pardon me for saying it, I don't think it's a good idea for a young man like you to go and live there all alone. If you were my son — you'll excuse me for saying it — you wouldn't sleep there one night, not if I had to go there myself and pull the big alarm bell that's on the roof!'

Malcolmson was amused and touched by her concern. [1] 'Don't worry about me, Mrs Witham. A man who is studying for a mathematics exam has got too much on his mind to be disturbed by mysterious "somethings". Mathematics is mysterious enough for me!'

Malcolmson went to the house with Mrs Witham, who was curious to see inside it, and after looking over the place, he decided to live in the great dining-room, which was big enough to eat and sleep in. Mrs Witham had kindly brought enough food from her kitchen to last a few days. Before leaving she said:

'The room is big and draughty. [2] You should have one of those big screens [3] round your bed at night. But — oh! — I would die myself if I were shut in with all kinds of "things"!'

When she had gone the cleaning woman arrived. Mrs Dempster said she wasn't afraid of any 'things'.

'Things is only rats and mice and beetles,' she said, 'and creaking doors. Look at this place — it's very old. Of course there are "things" here!'

1. **was amused... concern** : found her anxiety for his safety both humorous and moving.
2. **draughty** ['dra:fti] : cold because currents of air were coming through the windows and doors.
3. **screens** : moveable objects used to separate parts of a room for privacy.

Then she began to sweep and clean the place while Malcolmson went for a walk. By the time he got back it was night. He found the room clean, a fire burning in the old fireplace, and some of Mrs Witham's good food ready on the table for his dinner. After eating, he took out his books, put some wood on the fire, and started to do some real hard work. He studied until 11 o'clock, then made a cup of tea and had a rest. As he drank the hot tea and watched the shadows from the fire dancing round the great old room he enjoyed the feeling of isolation from the world. It was then that he began to notice the noise that the rats were making.

'That's strange,' he thought. 'They weren't making any noise before. Perhaps they were frightened by me, the light of the fire and the lamp, but now they're more courageous.'

How busy the rats were! They ran up and down behind the wall, over the ceiling, [1] and under the floor. Malcolmson smiled to himself and, stimulated by the tea, decided to have a good look at the room. Taking his lamp, he went all round and admired its beauty. There were some old pictures on the walls but they were covered with thick dust. Occasionally he saw the face of a rat, its bright eyes looking from a hole or crack in the wall. His attention was caught by the rope [2] of the great alarm bell. This rope hung down in a corner to the right of the fireplace. Sitting in a big oak chair by the fire, Malcolmson drank his last cup of tea, then returned to the table to start his work.

1. **ceiling** : surface of the top part of a room.
2. **rope** : strong thick cord, usually for tying things.

Suddenly he looked up. It was the hour before dawn and all was still and quiet. The rats had stopped their noise, the fire glowed a deep red. And there on the big oak chair sat an enormous rat, staring at him. He made a movement to scare it away but it didn't go. It showed its big white teeth angrily and its eyes shone cruelly in the lamplight. Amazed, he picked up the poker[1] from the fireplace and ran towards the creature to kill it. But with a squeak full of hate the rat jumped on the floor, ran up the rope of the alarm bell, and disappeared into the darkness. Strangely, at that moment the noise of the rats began again. Malcolmson couldn't continue his work after this, so he went to bed.

He slept so well that when Mrs Dempster came to prepare his breakfast he didn't wake up. After breakfast he took his books and some sandwiches and went out for a walk. He was out all day. On the way home he stopped to visit Mrs Witham, and told her the 'somethings' didn't worry him yet.

'Only the rats,' he added. 'They ran everywhere and made a lot of noise. There was one wicked devil that sat on my chair. I tried to kill him but he ran up the rope and escaped somewhere in the wall or ceiling — I couldn't see where.'

'A devil, a devil!' cried the landlady. 'Oh, be careful! Please don't laugh, young man!'

'Sorry, Mrs Witham, but it's so funny — the idea that the old devil himself was on the chair last night.'

That evening the noise of the rats began earlier. After dinner Malcolmson had a smoke and then he began to study. The rats

1. **poker** : metal bar used for moving the coals in the fire.

disturbed him more than before. How they ran up and down, how they squeaked and scratched! [1] And they became braver and braver until some of the bravest came out of their holes and ran across the floor. Occasionally Malcolmson made a sound like 'Tsh, tsh!' and hit the table to frighten them away. Despite the noise, he was absorbed in his work but suddenly he stopped, as on the night before, because he felt a sense of silence...

Instinctively he looked at the chair by the fire and a very strange sensation went through him. There on the big oak chair sat the same enormous rat, glaring at him with hostile eyes.

He threw a book at it but it stayed on the chair. So he took the poker again and chased it away. It ran up the rope again; and again, as soon as it had gone, the other rats began their noise. As before, Malcolmson couldn't see where exactly the big rat had disappeared because the green shade [2] on his lamp obscured the light there.

It was nearly midnight. He made his pot of tea and smoked a cigarette. Then he decided to find exactly where the rat had disappeared. Lighting another lamp, he placed it so that it shone into the corner of the fireplace. Next he got all his books ready to throw at the rat, and finally he put the end of the alarm bell rope under the lamp on his table.

'Hmm,' he thought. 'This is a strong, flexible rope — a good rope for hanging a man!'

He began his work again and soon got lost in it. Suddenly there was a slight movement of the rope and the lamp. He didn't

1. **scratched** : made a noise by scraping their claws on wood.
2. **shade** : part of the lamp that covers the light.

move. Looking along the rope, he saw the huge rat drop from it onto the chair. He took a book and threw it but the rat managed to avoid it. He threw two more books but missed each time. When he picked up another one the rat gave a squeak of fear. The book hit the animal hard. It gave a terrified squeal and, looking at Malcolmson with terrible malevolence, jumped onto the rope and ran up it like lightning. [1] This time he watched it carefully and saw it disappear through a hole in one of the pictures on the wall.

'The third picture from the fireplace,' said Malcolmson. 'I won't forget.'

While collecting the books he had thrown, the student looked at the titles. When he picked up the book that had terrified and hit the rat he became pale and started trembling with fear. It was the Bible his mother had given him.

He couldn't concentrate on his work for the rest of the night and went to bed just as dawn was breaking. [2] His sleep was heavy and full of strange dreams.

1. **like lightning** : very quickly.
2. **as dawn was breaking** : as the sun was starting to rise.

Go back to the text

FCE **1** **Choose the best answer A, B, C or D.**

1 Malcolm decided not to stay in the countryside or by the sea because

A ☐ he did not like being alone.

B ☐ he did not like either of these places.

C ☐ he liked the countryside and the sea so he would probably not study so much.

D ☐ he wanted to be alone and there were too many people in the countryside and at the seaside.

2 The landlady did not think it was a good idea for Malcolm to stay in the house because

A ☐ there was something wrong with it.

B ☐ young men should not live alone.

C ☐ the house was very old.

D ☐ it would be difficult to study there.

3 Mrs Dempster said that the strange things in the Judge's house were

A ☐ spirits and the ghost of the Judge.

B ☐ creations of the imagination.

C ☐ small animals.

D ☐ the noise of the wind.

4 The enormous rat sitting on the big oak chair surprised Malcolm the first time he saw it because

A ☐ it had bright eyes.

B ☐ he had never seen such a large rat before.

C ☐ it did not run away when he moved towards it.

D ☐ it was alone.

5 Mrs Witham thought that the enormous rat that Malcolm had seen was

A ☐ a devil.

B ☐ the Judge.

C ☐ just a rat.

D ☐ a ghost.

6 The second night Malcolm suddenly stopped studying because

- **A** ☐ the rats began making a lot of noise.
- **B** ☐ he felt the silence all around him.
- **C** ☐ he noticed the enormous rat looking at him.
- **D** ☐ the alarm bell began to ring.

7 The second night, Malcolm actually hit the enormous rat with

- **A** ☐ a mathematics book.
- **B** ☐ a Bible his mother had given him.
- **C** ☐ a poker.
- **D** ☐ the alarm bell rope.

8 After Malcolm hit the rat with a book it disappeared

- **A** ☐ up the rope of the alarm bell.
- **B** ☐ out the door.
- **C** ☐ through a hole in one of the paintings.
- **D** ☐ through a hole in the wall.

'He made up his mind to go somewhere quiet'

Look at this definition of **mind**:

The centre of consciousness which appears in the form of thoughts or feelings, or the totality of conscious and unconscious activities of the brain.

However, **mind** is also used in many idiomatic expressions. Look at these examples:

- Husband to wife: 'You paid $100 for a pair of gloves? **Are you out of your mind**?'
- Herbert: 'But you said you would come with me to the show!'
  Sylvia: 'Well, I am sorry, but **I've changed my mind**.'
- Ahmed: 'I don't know if I can come with you to the restaurant or not.'
  June: 'Well, you have to **make up your mind** soon because I have to book a table.'
- Mother to son: 'Stop looking out the window and **keep your mind on your** homework.'
- Jack: 'Samuel always **speaks his mind**. If he thinks you are wrong he will tell you.'

2 **Using the examples above to help you, match the expressions with mind (a-e) with their definitions (1-5).**

a. ☐ to keep your mind on something
b. ☐ to be out of your mind
c. ☐ to speak your mind
d. ☐ to make up your mind
e. ☐ to change your mind

1. to be crazy, mentally insane
2. to alter your opinion or decision
3. to come to a decision, to decide
4. to continue to concentrate on something
5. to say what you really think or believe

3 **Now complete the spaces with the correct expression. Make sure the verbs are in the correct tense.**

a. Please don't be offended, but I am going to .... I think you are an incompetent idiot.
b. You have to .... Do you want to marry me or Joseph?
c. It is hard to .... what I am doing with all this noise.
d. 'You must .... if you think I am going to work both Saturday and Sunday!'
e. 'I know that I said I would go with you to Spain, but .... I staying home with my family instead.
f. Jackson: 'Come on, Joe, ... ! You won't hurt my feelings.'
Joe: 'Well, your story is a bit boring.'
g. ....! Do you want steak or fish for dinner?

Before you go on

FCE **1 Listen to the beginning of Part Two and choose the best answer A, B or C.**

10

1 Malcolm surprised Mrs Dempster by asking her to

A ☐ to make him breakfast.
B ☐ to put his books in order.
C ☐ to clean the pictures on the wall.

2 Who was the man with Mrs Witham?

A ☐ Dr Maelstrom
B ☐ Dr Hornbill
C ☐ Dr Thornhill

3 When Malcolm said the rat was afraid of the Bible, Mrs Witham

A ☐ laughed.
B ☐ screamed.
C ☐ said nothing.

4 The doctor told Malcolm that the Judge had used the rope

A ☐ to hang his victims.
B ☐ to ring the bell.
C ☐ to tie up his victims.

5 Malcolm was glad to hear the noise of the rats again because

A ☐ they kept him from falling asleep.
B ☐ they kept him company while he studied.
C ☐ he had thought they might have been just a hallucination.

PART TWO

When Mrs Dempster woke him up late in the morning the first thing he said surprised her.

'Mrs Dempster, when I'm out today would you clean those pictures – especially the third one from the fireplace? I want to see what they are.'

Late that afternoon he visited Mrs Witham again and found a stranger with her. This was Dr Thornhill, who wanted to know what Malcolmson had seen in the old house. The student described exactly what had happened, and when he spoke about the rat's fear of the Bible, Mrs Witham screamed and needed a glass of brandy.

Dr Thornhill said to Malcolmson, 'I suppose you don't know what that rope is?'

Malcolmson said no and the doctor continued, 'It is the same rope which was used to hang all the victims of the Judge's cruelty.'

Again Mrs Witham screamed. When she had recovered and Malcolmson had gone home she asked the doctor why he had told the young man about the rope. 'You've put horrible ideas into that poor boy's head,' she added.

'My dear Mrs Witham,' said the doctor, 'I did it intentionally to fix the rope in his mind. He may have a strange hallucination during the night and I want him to pull that rope. I'm going to bed late tonight. I'll listen very carefully and if the alarm bell rings I may be in time to help him.'

'Oh Doctor, what do you mean?'

'I mean this: we are going to get a surprise before morning.'

When Malcolmson arrived home he was pleased to see that the room was bright with a fire and a lamp. The evening was cold for April and a strong wind was blowing. It looked as though a storm was coming. After his arrival the noise of the rats stopped, but it began again after a few minutes. He was happy to hear them; they were like companions now. Only the reading-lamp was lit, so the corner where the rope hung was dark. The student ate his dinner hungrily, smoked, and sat down to work. After an hour the wind had become a storm which made the house shake. The storm roared [1] in the chimney and made strange sounds in the empty rooms and corridors. Even the rope moved slightly. Remembering the doctor's words, Malcolmson got up and examined it. He took it in his hand, thinking about the Judge's victims, and as the bell moved on the roof the rope also moved. But soon there was a sort of tremor in the rope; something was moving along it.

END

1. **roared** : made a loud noise.

Looking up, Malcolmson saw the great rat coming slowly down towards him. He let go of the rope and jumped away. The rat ran back up the rope and disappeared. Then it suddenly became clear to Malcolmson that he hadn't investigated the third picture. He lit the second lamp, looked at the picture, and jumped so quickly he nearly dropped the lamp. His face was as white as a ghost and his legs trembled.

The picture was of a judge dressed in his scarlet robes. [1] His face was evil and vindicative. There was a cruel, cunning look in it. The red nose was like the beak of a falcon, the mouth sensual, and the eyes were unusually brilliant with a terribly malignant expression. Malcolmson grew cold when he recognized the eyes of the great rat! And with a sensation of horror he saw that the Judge in the picture was sitting in a high, oak chair on the right of the fireplace where, in the corner, a rope hung from the ceiling. It was the same room where Malcolmson stood and he looked round as if expecting to see a strange presence behind him. And when he looked he saw... the rat in the Judge's armchair looking at him with the Judge's malignant eyes. With a loud cry he dropped the lamp. Now all was silent, except for the storm howling [2] outside.

Luckily the lamp wasn't broken. Malcolmson picked it up and put it out. [3] Wiping the sweat from his face, [4] he tried to think for a moment.

1. **scarlet robes** : long, bright red clothes traditionally worn by judges.
2. **howling** : making a long sad call, like the sound that wolves make.
3. **put it out** : extinguished it.
4. **wiping... face** : cleaning the sweat (caused by fear) from his face, with his hand or handkerchief.

'If I continue like this I'll go crazy,' he said to himself. 'This must stop! My nerves are in a bad state and I didn't realize it. But it's all right now.'

He made a strong glass of brandy and water and sat down, determined to continue his work. Nearly an hour passed before he looked up from his book, disturbed by the sudden stillness. Outside the wind howled and roared louder than ever and the rain crashed against the windows. But inside it was quiet. Malcolmson listened carefully and heard squeaking in the corner where the rope hung. It was the big rat again, and it was biting the rope. As the student watched, the rope broke and fell on the floor, while the rat remained hanging on the end it had bitten, which began to swing. The young man suddenly felt terror as he realized that now he couldn't pull the rope and call for help. But this changed to fierce anger and he threw his book at the rat. The animal dropped onto the floor, but managed to avoid the book. Malcolmson instantly ran towards it but it disappeared in the shadows of the room.

'If it's the last thing I do I'll hunt and catch the wicked devil,' he thought.

He took off the green shade of the lamp and light filled the room. Now from where he stood he could see the third picture on the wall very clearly. He rubbed his eyes [1] in surprise, and then a great fear came over him. The picture was the same as before — but the figure of the Judge had disappeared!

Cold with horror, he turned slowly round; then he began to tremble uncontrollably and became so weak he couldn't move.

1. **rubbed his eyes** : pressed and moved his fingers on his eyes.

On the great oak chair sat the Judge in his scarlet robes. His vindicative eyes glared at the student and he smiled a cruel smile as he began to raise a black cap in his hands. Through the noise of the storm Malcolmson could hear the striking of the great clock in the market square in Benchurch. It was midnight. He stood there for what seemed an eternity, still as a statue, his eyes wide open with terror. And at the last stroke of midnight the Judge put the black cap on his head.

Slowly the Judge stood up and took the rope which lay on the floor. Slowly he began to tie one end of it into a noose.[1] Then he started to move across the room until he stood in front of the door, blocking Malcolmson's escape. All the time he fixed his eyes on the young student, who seemed to be hypnotized. Coming slowly towards him, the Judge threw the noose to catch him round the neck. But with an immense effort Malcolmson moved quickly to one side and the noose fell on the floor. Again the Judge tried to catch him in the noose and again he just managed to escape. This was repeated many times, the Judge playing with him like a cat plays with a mouse.

Finally, in a climax of despair, the student glanced quickly around to see how he could escape. And he saw that the alarm bell rope near the ceiling was covered with rats. More and more of them were coming through the hole in the ceiling and running up and down the rope so that with their weight the bell was beginning to swing. Then Malcolmson heard a distant clang[2] as the bell sounded on the roof. The Judge looked up with an

1. **noose** : circular piece of rope used for hanging.
2. **clang** : metallic ringing sound.

· D ·

expression of diabolical anger on his face. Thunder crashed above the house as he held open the noose and came close to Malcolmson. The student seemed paralysed by the Judge's close presence and stood rigid as a corpse. He felt the Judge's icy fingers tightening the rope round his neck. The noose tightened... tightened... Then the Judge carried the rigid student to the oak chair and stood him on it. As the Judge got onto the chair and put up his hand to take the end of the swinging rope the rats ran away in fear and disappeared. In a moment the Judge tied the end of the noose to the bell rope, got off the chair, and pulled it from under Malcolmson's feet.

The bell of the Judge's house soon brought a crowd of people hurrying there with lights and torches. They knocked loudly but there was no reply. Then they broke down the door and ran into the great dining room, led by Dr Thornhill. There at the end of the rope in the corner hung the body of the young student, and on the face of the Judge in the picture there was a malignant smile.

Go back to the text

1 Answer the following questions.

a. Why did Dr Thornhill tell Malcolm about the rope?

b. Why did the third picture horrify Malcolm when he first looked at it?

c. What did the rat and the Judge have in common?

d. Why did the rat bite off the rope?

e. How did the third picture change?

f. What sign did the Judge give that Malcolm had been sentenced to death?

g. Why did the alarm bell ring?

'He felt the Judge's icy fingers tightening the rope round his neck'

Verbs of perception like ***notice, see, watch, feel, smell, hear*** and ***listen to*** can be followed by either an infinitive (without to) or the present participle (-ing).

The **infinitive** is used to talk about short, immediate or complete actions. Look at these examples:

- We ***saw*** her ***run*** into the room and fall onto the floor.
- They ***heard*** the bell ***ring*** twice.

The **present participle** is used to talk about longer action or something that continued. Look at these examples:

- I ***heard*** her ***singing*** a beautiful song.
- He ***felt*** the Judge ***tightening*** the rope.

2 In the following sentences place the verb in brackets in the correct form.

Examples:

He was terrified, he saw the Judge (walk) ***walking*** towards him with a rope in his hand.

Last night I heard someone (jump) ***jumping*** up and down in the room above mine, which made it impossible for me to sleep.

a. Jack isn't home. Did you see him (*go*) .... out?

b. I heard him (*open*) .... the front door and (*run*) .... up the stairs.

c. Last night I noticed a strange man (*stand*) .... in front of my house.

d. I think I hear a rat (*squeak*) ....

e. You can't deny it! I heard you (*say*) .... that you were coming to Jane's party.

f. Everybody was listening to Harold (*tell*) .... a joke when I walked into the room.

g. Oh no! I can smell the roast (*burn*) .... Go and turn off the oven.

h. I fell asleep on the grass, and I did not wake until an hour later when I felt the rain (*fall*) .... on my face.

3 Which of the adjectives in the box describe these characters? Write them in the appropriate column.

cruel	practical	timid	hard-working		
vindictive	malignant	humorous	superstitious		
clever	hysterical	realistic	kind	motherly	friendly
studious	cheerful	curious	efficient	cunning	

Malcolmson	Mrs Witham	Mrs Dempster	The Judge

4 Look at the people/things in the box below. What function do they have in the story? Put them in the appropriate column and explain how. You may use some of them more than once.

the big rat **Dr Thornhill** **the storm** **Mr Carnford** **the rope** **Mrs Dempster** **the house** **Mrs Witham** **the picture**

function	who/what?	how?
symbol of the Judge's cruelty		
creates atmosphere of suspense/mystery	1. Mr Carnford	says people have a 'prejudice' about the house and nobody wants to live there
creates atmosphere of horror/terror	1. the house	large, old, empty and isolated; makes noises; has rats and other 'things'
adds humour or normality		

Why did I tell him about the rope?

5 Dr Thornhill feels very bad about Malcolm's death. He feels as if he is to blame in part.
Pretend you are Dr Thornhill and write in your diary what happened to Malcolm and why you feel that you are to blame.
Include the following information in your diary entry:

- why Malcolm came to Benchurch
- where he decided to live
- how Malcolm learned about the Judge
- what you said to Malcolm
- why Malcolm was susceptible to hallucinations

You can begin like this:

6th April 1898

A few days ago a young man named Malcolm Malcolmson came to our town to . . .

FCE **1** **Choose the correct answer A, B, C or D.**

The Monkey's Paw

1 An old fakir put a spell on the monkey's paw to show that

- **A** ☐ he was the best magician in India.
- **B** ☐ he could interfere with fate whenever he wanted.
- **C** ☐ it was not possible to interfere with fate.
- **D** ☐ people should not try to interfere with fate.

2 Sergeant Major Morris said that the wishes happened

- **A** ☐ after several years.
- **B** ☐ in strange and unexpected ways.
- **C** ☐ naturally so that people thought they were just coincidences.
- **D** ☐ only if you really believed in the powers of the monkey's paw.

3 What did Herbert see in the fire after his father had made his wish?

- **A** ☐ A face that looked like Sergeant Major Morris.
- **B** ☐ A monkey's paw that seemed to move.
- **C** ☐ A face that looked like a monkey.
- **D** ☐ Something that looked like a bag of money.

4 Maw and Meggins gave the Whites £200 because

- **A** ☐ Herbert had worked well for them and they wished to compensate the Whites for his death.
- **B** ☐ they felt responsible for his death.
- **C** ☐ the law said that they had to give money to Mr and Mrs White.
- **D** ☐ they had not yet paid Herbert for two months of work.

5 Mr White did not want to wish for Herbert's return because

- **A** ☐ he did not think it was right to change fate.
- **B** ☐ Herbert's body had been crushed by the machinery.
- **C** ☐ he did not believe the monkey paw could grant wishes and so he did not want his wife to be disappointed.
- **D** ☐ he wanted to use the last two wishes for himself.

The Phantom Coach

1 James Murray had told only one person his story because

- A ☐ he himself was not really sure he had seen it.
- B ☐ it was such a terrifying experience that he tried not to think about it.
- C ☐ he had promised his wife that he would not talk about it.
- D ☐ he did not want anyone to try and convince him that it hadn't really happened.

2 What did the master of the house study?

- A ☐ the supernatural
- B ☐ chemistry
- C ☐ old systems of philosophy
- D ☐ local legends

3 The master of the house lived alone in a remote part of England because

- A ☐ he did not like to receive guests.
- B ☐ he did not like the city.
- C ☐ his fellow scientists and philosophers had destroyed his reputation.
- D ☐ he wanted to investigate the story of the phantom coach.

4 When did James Murray realize that he was in the phantom coach?

- A ☐ When he realized that it was so cold inside.
- B ☐ When he saw the coach on the steep dangerous road.
- C ☐ When he saw the signpost.
- D ☐ When he looked into the faces of the other passengers.

5 How did James Murray say that he had fallen over the precipice?

- A ☐ The phantom coach went through the broken wall at the signpost.
- B ☐ It so dark that, as he was walking, he walked through the broken wall.
- C ☐ He opened the door of the phantom coach and threw himself out.
- D ☐ The phantom coach had knocked him over as he was walking along the path.

The Fall of the House of Usher

1 How did the narrator know Roderick Usher?

A ☐ He and Roderick Usher were neighbours.
B ☐ The narrator was Madeline's physician.
C ☐ They had been childhood friends.
D ☐ The narrator was a friend of Roderick's family.

2 What were the symptoms of Roderick Usher's disease?

A ☐ an extreme acuteness of the senses
B ☐ a strange fear of his house and its influence on him and his family
C ☐ apathy and catalepsy
D ☐ terrible headaches

3 Roderick Usher had the strange belief that his family house

A ☐ was going to fall down very soon.
B ☐ had feelings and had made him what he was.
C ☐ had ghosts in it.
D ☐ would never be destroyed.

4 The narrator read his friend a novel about Ethelred who

A ☐ kills a dragon.
B ☐ buries his sister alive.
C ☐ lives in a house full of ghosts.
D ☐ is killed by a terrible dragon.

5 The narrator noticed that as he read the book 'Mad Trist' that

A ☐ Roderick Usher seemed to feel better.
B ☐ he could hear in the house the terrible sounds described in the book.
C ☐ the storm outside got even worse.
D ☐ the storm outside seemed to calm down.

The Judge's House

1 Malcolm Malcolmson went to Benchurch

A ☐ to take a holiday.
B ☐ to visit some relatives.
C ☐ to study for his mathematics examination.
D ☐ to visit some friends.

2 Why did the people of Benchurch think there was something wrong with the Judge's House?

A ☐ A cruel judge had lived there.
B ☐ A cruel judge had killed many people there.
C ☐ It was full of rats.
D ☐ It was very old and looked like a fortified house.

3 What disturbed Malcolm during his first night in the Judge's House?

A ☐ the draught
B ☐ the wind
C ☐ the total silence
D ☐ the rats

4 How did Malcolm finally terrify the big rat?

A ☐ He threw his Bible at it.
B ☐ He threw his mathematics book at it.
C ☐ He hit the table.
D ☐ He yelled.

5 Dr Thornhill told Malcolm about the rope because

A ☐ he thought Malcolm might need help during the night.
B ☐ he wanted to frighten Malcolm away from the house.
C ☐ he thought Malcolm might be interested in the history of the town.
D ☐ Malcolm seemed so frightened by it.

2 Who said what and why?

Below are some quotations from some of the characters who feature in the four stories. Match each quotation to the correct character and then match it to reason why he said it. Write the letter that represents each character in the spaces in the first column and the letter of the reason why in the second.

Who

Mr White (W)

James Murray (J)

Roderick Usher (R)

Malcolm Malcolmson (M)

What

Who	Why		
		1	My nerves are in a bad state and I didn't realize it.
		2	How do you do it?
		3	The right of self-preservation.
		4	I am not afraid of danger but I'm afraid of its effect — terror.
		5	The third picture from the fireplace. I won't forget.
		6	It's foolish and wicked.
		7	It seems to me I've got all I want.
		8	This is real winter weather.

Why

a. He is saying what he thinks of wishing for his son's return from the dead.

b. He is telling the master of house how he is justified in entering the house uninvited.

c. He is talking about how he will die.

d. He is trying to start up a conversation.

e. He is noting where the giant rat escaped.

f. He is explaining why he does not know what to wish for.

g. He says this because he thinks his fear is ridiculous.

h. He wants to know how to make a wish with the monkey's paw.

FCE 3 Write the answer to one of the questions below. Write your answer in 120-180 words in an appropriate style.

1 You have decided to enter a short story competition. All stories must have a ghost or horror theme. Your story must **end** with the following words.
I have never been so afraid in my life.
Write your **story**.

2 'An important element of Gothic literature is how the setting helps create an atmosphere of suspense' Write a **composition** commenting on the setting of the stories you have read and say what role it has in building suspense. Use examples from the four stories to illustrate your point of view.

Key to Exit Test

1 The Monkey's Paw
1.D 2.C 3.C 4.A 5.B

The Phantom Coach
1.D 2.A 3.C 4.D 5.A

The Fall of the House of Usher
1.C 2.A 3.B 4.A 5.B

The Judge's House
1.C 2.B 3.D 4.A 5.A

2

	Who	Why
1.	M	g
2.	W	h
3.	J	b
4.	R	c
5.	M	e
6.	W	a
7.	W	f
8.	J	d

3 Open answers